# Introduction to Sorani Kurdish

## The Principal Kurdish Dialect Spoken in the Regions of Northern Iraq and Western Iran

Livingston T. Merchant, PhD

*Advisory editor: Paiman Ramazan*
*Karwan Qadir and Zina Chaqmaqchee*

UNIVERSITY OF RAPARIN

1

ISBN-13: 978-1483969268

# Table of Contents

## Preface

This book is primarily intended as a language learning tool for foreigners coming to the provinces under the jurisdiction of the Kurdistan Regional Government in Northern Iraq. It contains brief historical, cultural and political notes to help the learner understand the social environment of the Sorani dialect. It is designed so that it may be used with the help of a native-speaking Kurdish mentor.

It is important to understand that the aim of the book is ***communication skills***, not linguistic expertise. The structure of the language is introduced simply and in small doses. Grammar can best be absorbed by learning word patterns that will give the learner the ability to generate new phrases. A detailed study of grammar is best left until after the mastery of the basics of communications.

For a number of reasons, there is no standard Kurdish language or even a standard Sorani dialect. Variations occur from region to region and even from speaker to speaker. I have used as a standard the speech of educated speakers from the province of Sulaymaniye. Other Kurdish speakers will find many "mistakes" in the spoken forms, the vocabulary, and the pronunciation of the Kurdish content of this book. These "mistakes" are merely witness to the fact that there is no "correct" form of the language.

# Introduction: The Kurdish people and their language

## A. The origins and geographical distribution of the Kurdish people

The ancestors of the modern-day Kurds have occupied their lands for more than two thousand years and are the descendants of Indo-Iranian and other peoples including the Medes, the ancient collaborators in the building of the early Persian Empire. Since the fall of the Ottoman Empire in the early twentieth century, the Kurds have been divided among four separate states: Turkey, Iraq, Iran and Syria.

The only region with an autonomous Kurdish government is in northern Iraq. The Kurdistan Regional Government in Iraq has jurisdiction over an area approximately the size of the Netherlands with a population of about five million people. This region is in a federation with the rest of Iraq, but maintains its own executive, legislative, and judicial organs. It also has diplomatic relations with a number of other countries and maintains strong independent security and military forces.

The political divisions of the modern-day Kurds directly affect their lack of linguistic unity. This political fragmentation naturally has impeded any movement toward the creation of a standard Kurdish language. A unified standard language is usually the product of a unified political state.

## B. The Kurdish language and its dialects.

Kurdish is made up of a group of dialects belonging to the eastern branch of the Indo-European family of languages along with Russian, Latvian, Hindi, Urdu, Marathi and a number of other modern Eurasian languages. It resembles closely modern Persian or Farsi.

Sorani is spoken by ten or more million Kurds living in Iraq and Iran and is the dominant dialect in the cities Hewler (Erbil), Dohuk and Sulaymaniye and their surrounding regions. It is also spoken in the "disputed" territories around Kirkuk and Mosul, where Kurdish, Arab and Turkmen populations are mixed. Today the majority of Kurdish speakers lives in Turkey and speaks several dialects, the most wide-spread of which is Kurmanci. Speakers of Sorani and Kurmanci can only understand each other with great difficulty, but learning Sorani will facilitate the learning of Kurmanci and other related dialects.

## C. A comment on the sensitive word "Kurdistan"

**Iraqi Kurdistan: the area governed by the Kurdish Regional Government**

8

"Kurdistan" is a word which is politically sensitive, even explosive, and a foreigner would be wise to exercise caution in using it. It can mean very different things to different people. In Iraq it refers formally to the three provinces Erbil (Hewler), Dohuk and Sulaymaniye, which are governed by the Kurdistan Regional Government. The use of the word Kurdistan in this book refers to this regional entity, and no political significance is intended.

In Iraq the Kurdish speaking areas are sometimes referred to as Southern Kurdistan. To the West in Syria, to the North in Turkey, and to the East in Iran lie areas inhabited by millions of other Kurdish speakers. Many Kurds refer to these regions as parts of Kurdistan. To the governments and many of the people of these countries, this presents the specter of separatist movements that could divide their national territories.

# The Kurdo-Arabic alphabet and its transliteration

The Sorani dialect is normally written in a version of Arabic script with variations to represent Kurdish sounds. Unlike Arabic, Kurdish writing indicates almost all the vowels, and not just the consonants. Because dialects and speakers differ, the written language, either in the Kurdo-Arabic script or the Romanized script known as Latini, is only an approximation of the spoken language.

Latin letters are used in the transliteration of the Sorani words in this text. Following this chart will give the reader an approximation of Sorani sounds, but a good pronunciation of the language can only be learned from a Sorani speaker or from recordings.

|   |   | Approximate English sound |
|---|---|---|
| Vowels | | |
| a | ە | a as in bat; unstressed at the end of a word, a as in Flora |
| â | ١ | a as in above |
| e | ە | e as in bet; unstressed at the end of a word, a as in Flora |
| ê | ێ | a as in late |
| i | * | i as in bit; * i is not written in the Kurdo-Arabic alphabet. |
| î | ى | i as in elite |
| o | ۆ | o as in wrote |

| u | و | u as in put |
|---|---|---|
| û | وو | oo as in pool |
| Diphthongs | | |
| aw | او | a combination of the vowels a + u |
| âw | ئو | a combination of the vowels â + u |
| ew | ەو | a combination of the vowels e + u |
| êw | يّو | a combination of the vowels ê + u |
| Consonants | | |
| a' | ع | not found in English: a voiced glottal stop |
| b | ب | b |
| ç | چ | ch as in church |
| d | د | d |
| f | ف | f |
| g | گ | g as in gone |
| gh | غ | not found in English; close to Parisian r |
| h | ە | h |
| <u>h</u> | ح | <u>h</u> is a slightly stronger fricative than h. |
| j | ج | j as in jelly |
| k | ک | k |
| l | ل | l as in pill |
| ll | لّ | ll as in all. |
| m | م | m |
| n | ن | n |
| p | پ | p |
| q | ق | a guttural k not found in English. |
| r | ر | a tongue tap behind the teeth |

| rr | ڕ | as the trilled r in Spanish carro |
|---|---|---|
| s | س | s |
| ş | ش | sh |
| t | ت | t |
| v | ڤ | v |
| w/u | و | w/u |
| x | خ | ch as in German Bach or Scottish loch |
| y | ی | y |
| z | ز | z |
| zh | ژ | g as in beige |

In the lessons, the dialogs and some grammar examples are given both in the Kurdo-Arabic alphabet and in the Romanized form, Latini. The former is intended for the convenience of a Kurdish tutor or friend who is reading the texts aloud. It is not expected that a student will master the Sorani alphabet at the beginning of his or her study.

## A word about stress

Sorani nouns and adjectives are usually stressed on the last syllable of their root, and the stress remains on that syllable even with the addition of one or more endings. The stress pattern in verbs is complex. The beginner should acquire these by learning the dialogs and listening to native speakers.

## Acknowledgements

Completing this book would not have been possible without the support of the University of Raparin, its President Dr. Mohammed Ali Abdulla, and Dr. Bahzad Hamad, formerly the university's Vice-President.

Mamosta Paiman Ramazan, Director of Publicity and Publications of the University of Raparin, was the advisory editor of this book. She went over every word, correcting errors and suggesting many improvements.

Mamosta Karwan Qadir, teacher of English in the school system in Ranya, helped with the translations from English to Kurdish. His understanding of both English and Kurdish and his abilities in communication skills have made him an ideal assistant.

Mamosta Zina Çaqmaqchee, an instructor at Soran University, reviewed the text and made many suggestions on the usage and orthography of the Sorani language.

The grammar notes are simplified and abbreviated paradigms that follow the patterns of W.H. Thackston, (2006) *Sorani Kurdish: Reference Grammar, Selected Reading, and Vocabulary*, from Iranian Studies at Harvard University, http://www.fas.harvard.edu/~iranian/Sorani/index.html.

Finally, without the encouragement and proofreading skills of my wife, Çiğdem Merchant, this project would never have been completed.

# Lesson 1 - Meeting in the Bazaar

Two young Kurdish friends meet in the street and greet each other. Sarhad, has a phone shop in the bazaar. Rêbar runs a small computer repair shop. They greet each other and want to talk, but they have no time. Serhad is late for an appointment and must hurry. They say goodbye, expecting to meet again the next day.

## Sarhad

| | | |
|---|---|---|
| Beyânît bâş. | Good morning. | به يانيت |
| Çonî? | How are you? | باش، جۆنى ؟ |

## Rêbar

| | | |
|---|---|---|
| Bâşim, Sarhad. | I'm fine, Sarhad. | باشم سه ر هه د. |
| Supâs. To bâşît? | Thank you. How are you? | سوپاس. تۆ باشيت؟ |

## Serhad

| | | |
|---|---|---|
| Miniş bâşim, bellâm kemêk dwâdekewim. | I'm fine also, but I'm a little late. | منيش باشم، به‌ڵام که مێک دوا ده که وم. |

14

| Pewîste êstâ birrom. | I must go now. | پێویسته ئێستا بڕۆم. |
| Sibey detbinmewe. Xwâ âfîz. | I will see you tomorrow. Goodbye. | سبهی ده تبینمه وه، خواحافیز. |

## Rêbar

| Serçâwim.* | Farewell. | سه رجاوم. |

*Serçâwim is an expression used to say farewell and roughly translates[you are] "on my eyes". It is also used for answering a request for a favor or help. Kurds say Serçâwim when asked a favor to indicate acceptance.

Note: The polite language of greetings and farewells in Kurdish is formal and stylized, as in most languages.

## Words and phrases

| | |
|---|---|
| beyânî | morning |
| bâş | good |
| çonî | how are you |
| supâs | thank you |
| bâşim | I'm well |
| to | you (singular) |
| minîş | I also |
| bellâm | but |
| kemêk | a little |
| dwâdekewim | I'm late |
| pewîste | must |

| | |
|---|---|
| **êstâ** | now |
| **birrom** | I go |
| **min** | I |
| **sibey** | tomorrow |
| **detbinmewe** | I will see |
| **xwâ** | god or Allah |
| <u>**h**</u>**afîz** | protect |
| **serçâw** | goodbye |

## To be or not to be, expressing "to be", "there is"

When personal pronoun endings are added to nouns and adjectives, they take the place of the English verb "to be". The negative of the verb to be has a special form that follows a noun or adjective, with the meaning "am not", "is not", "there is no", "are not", "there are no".

Pronoun endings attached to a noun or adjective ending in a consonant:

| | |
|---|---|
| I | -im |
| you (sg.) | -ît |
| he/she/it | -a |
| we | -în |
| you (pl.) | -in |
| they | -in |

Pronoun endings attached to a noun or adjective ending in a vowel:

| I | -m |
|---|---|
| you (sg.) | -yt |
| he/she/it | -ya |
| we | -yn |
| you (pl.) | -n |
| they | -n |

The negative form of the verb "to be" :

| I | niyim |
|---|---|
| you (sg.) | niyît |
| he/she/it | niya |
| we | niyîn |
| you (pl.) | niyin |
| they | niyin |

**Examples**

| Âya to bâşî? | Are you well? |
|---|---|
| Min bâşim. | I am well. |
| Eme kogâka niya. | This is not the store. |
| Âya to Kurdî? | Are you Kurdish? |
| Hiç kitêbêk lewêda niye. | There are no books there. |

**Words and phrases**

| **âya** | introduces a question |
|---|---|
| **eme** | this |
| **koga** | store |

17

| | |
|---|---|
| **hiç** | none, no, any |
| **kitêb** | book |
| **lewê** | there |

## Translate into English.

Beyânît bâş. Çonît?
Bâşim. Supâs. To çonît?
Minîş bâşim. Pewîste êstâ birrom.
Xwâ âfîz.
Serçâw.

## Translate into Kurdish

Good morning.
How are you ?
I am well. And you?
I must go. Farewell.

# Lesson 2 - An Evening Visit

It is about 8 p.m., and a young teacher, Nîhâd, passes by the home of his university professor, Dr. Azâd. He knocks on the door to pay his respects. Dr. Azâd welcomes him and invites him in. It is the custom in traditional homes to remove one's shoes before entering. Seating is often on the floor.

Dr. Azad brings Nîhâd a glass of cold water, the traditional offering to every guest. He then asks if he will take anything to drink, but Nîhâd politely declines, and saying that he is tired and should go home. They bid each other good night.

## Dr. Azâd

| | | |
|---|---|---|
| Mâmostâ* Nîhâd, êwâre bâş. | Mamosta Nihad, good evening. | مامۆستا نیهاد نێواره باش. |
| Baxêrbêyt. Tikâye were zhûrewe. | Welcome. Please come in. | به خێربێیت ، تکایه وه ره ژووره وه. |

## Nîhâd

| | | |
|---|---|---|
| Supâs, diktor Âzâd. Bâşe ke lêrey.** | Thank you, Dr. Azad. It is good to be here. | سوپاس د کتۆر ئازاد ، باشه که لێره‌ی. |

## Dr. Azâd

| Fermû hendê âwî sârd. | Please have some cold water. | فەرموو هەندئ ئاوى سارد. |
| Qâwe yân çâ axoytewe ? | Would you care for coffee or tea? | قاوه یان چا ئه وّیتهوه؟ |

## Nîhâd

| Nâ, supâs. Kemêk mândûm. Pewîste birrom. | Thank you, no. I am a little tired. I should go. | نا سوپاس، کە مێک ماندووم، پیویستە برۆم. |

## Dr Azâd

| Şew şâd. Xwâ âgâdârit bê. | Good night. God take care of you. | شەو و شاد ، خوا ئاگادارتبیّ. |

*Mâmostâ means "teacher", and it is used as a term of respect even in conversation between friends. Similarly, Kâk, "sir" or "mister" is commonly used before first name of friends, bus drivers, waiters, strangers, etc. in common conversation. If a person has a doctor's degree, whether medical or academic, the word diktor, "doctor", is almost always used to address him or her in normal conversation.

** **Bâşe ke lêrey**. "It is good to be here." This is a set formal response to being welcomed.

## Words and phrases

| | |
|---|---|
| **mâmostâ** | teacher |
| **êwâre bâş** | good evening. |
| **bâxêrbêy** | welcome |
| **tikâye** | please |
| **were zhûrewe** | come in |
| **supâs** | thank you |
| **diktor** | doctor |
| **bâşe** | it is good |
| **ke** | that |
| **lêre** | here |
| **fermû** | please have |
| **hendê** | some |
| **âw** | water |
| **sârd** | cold |
| **qâwe** | coffee |
| **yân** | or |
| **çâ** | tea |
| **nâ, supâs** | no, thank you |
| **kemêk** | a little |
| **mândûm** | I am tired. |
| **pewîste** | should |
| **birrom** | I go |
| **şew** | night |
| **şâd** | happy |
| **âgâdârît bê** | may [God] take care |

# Demonstrative adjectives and pronouns

Demonstrative adjectives: **am**, "this/these" and **aw**, "that/those" precede the noun, and the noun takes the following endings: **-e** after a singular noun ending in a consonant, **-ye** after a singular noun ending in a vowel, **-âne** after a plural noun ending in consonant, and **-yâne** after a plural noun ending in a vowel.

## Examples

| | |
|---|---|
| am pyâwe | this man |
| am pyâwâne | these men |
| am dergâye | this door |
| am dergâyâne | these doors |
| aw zhine | that woman |
| aw zhinâne | those women |
| aw zânkoye | that university |
| aw dergâyâne | those doors |
| am kitêbe bâşe. | This book is good. |

Demonstrative pronouns: **ame**, "this", **amâne**, "these" **awe**, "that", **awâne**, "those". These pronouns are stressed on the final **e**.

## Examples

| | |
|---|---|
| Awe le êrane | That is in Iran. |
| Awâne jwânin. | Those are beautiful. |

22

| | |
|---|---|
| Ame rêgâkeye bo bâxeke. | This is the way to the park. |
| Amâne birâkânmin. | These are my brothers. |
| Awe şâxe qendîle. | That is Qandil mountain. |

## Translate into English.

Beyânît bâş. Çonît?
Bâşim. Supâs. To çonît?
Baxêrbêyt. Tikâye were zhûrewe.
Supâs. Bâşe ke lêrey.
Sibey detbinmewe. Xwâ âfîz.
Şew şâd.


## Translate into Kurdish.

Good evening. Come in.
How are you?
I am a little tired
Are you tired?
Have some cold water.
Have some tea.
Good night.

# Lesson 3 - Where Are You From?

John has arrived at the Language Center of Raparin University in Qaladze, where he has just begun teaching English. One day he walks into a park near the campus. Omed, a student, is sitting on a bench, and invites John to talk. Omed asks if they can speak in Kurdish, but John replies that he really cannot. Omêd asks John's nationality. He explains he was born in America,, but his mother is French. Therefore he speaks only English and French. John wants to learn Kurdish and wonders if Omed could help him. Omed is glad to.

## Omêd

| | | |
|---|---|---|
| Âya be kurdî qise dekeyt? | Excuse me, do you speak Kurdish? | ئایا به کوردی قسه ده که یت؟ |

## John

| | | |
|---|---|---|
| Nâ. Min tenhâ be înglîzî u ferensî qise dekem. | No. I only speak English and French. | نا،من ته نها به ئینگلیزی و فه رهنسی قسه ده که م. |

**Omêd**

| Le kwewe hâtûy? | Where are you from? | له کوێوه هاتووی؟ |
| Âya to Emirîkî? | Are you American? | ئایا تۆئەمریکی |

**John**

| Min Emirîkîm u le Emirîkâ le dâyk bûm. Boye be Înglîzî qise dekem. | I am American. I was born in America, so I speak English. | من ئەمریکیم وله ئەمریکا له دایک بووم. بۆیه به ئینگلیزی قسه ده کەم. |
| Dâyîkim ferensîye. Boye be ferensî qise dekem. | My mother is French. That is why I speak French. | دایکم ف ه ر ه نسیه ، بۆیه به فەرهنسی قسه ده که م. |
| Detwânim kemêk be kurdî qise bikem, bellâm be tewâwi nâ. | I can speak a little Kurdish, but not enough. | ده توانم کەمێک به کوردی قسه بکه م، به لام به ته ت واوی نا. |
| Âya detwânît yârmetîm deyt be kurdî qise bikem? | Could you help me to speak Kurdish? | ئایه    ده توانیت، یارمه تیم   ده یت به کوردی قسه بکەم؟ |

**Omêd**

| Min xoşhâllim be yârmetî dânit | I would be glad to help you. | من خۆشحاڵم به یارمەتی دانت. |

## Words and phrases

| | |
|---:|---|
| **be kurdî** | in Kurdish |
| **qise dekeyt** | you speak |
| **tenhâ** | only |
| **înglîzî** | English |
| **ferensî** | French |
| **le kwêwe** | from |
| **hâtûy** | you come |
| **emirîkî** | American |
| **le** | in |
| **le dâyk bûm** | I was born |
| **emirîkâ** | America |
| **boye** | therefore, so |
| **qise dekem** | I speak |
| **dâyîkim** | my mother |
| **ferensî** | is French |
| **detwânim** | I can |
| **bellâm** | but |
| **tewâw** | enough |
| **detwânî** | you could |
| **yârmetîm** | help me |
| **bideyt** | give |
| **xoşhâllim** | I am glad |
| **yârmetî dânit** | help you |

## Nouns

Nouns in Sorani have three states: 1. The absolute state, which is the form found in the dictionary listing and which is used to make general statements, such as "milk is white", "sugar is sweet", etc. 2. The indefinite state, a noun which in English would be marked by "a/an", "some", "any": "a man", "an apple", "any card in the deck". 3. The definite state, a noun which in English would be marked by "the", "this", "that": "the army", "this table", "the mountains".

The absolute state of the noun is the root of the noun without any endings.

| | |
|---|---|
| pyâw | man |
| dergâ | door |
| zânko | university |

The singular of the indefinite state of the noun is formed by adding **-ek** to the absolute form of the noun if it ends in a consonant and **-yek** if it ends in a vowel. These endings are not stressed.

| | |
|---|---|
| pyâwek | a man |
| dergâyek | a door |
| zânkoyek | a university |

The plural of the indefinite state of the noun is formed by adding **-ân** to the absolute form of the noun if it ends in a consonant and **-yân** if it ends in a vowel. This ending is stressed.

|  |  |
|---|---|
| pyâwân | men |
| dergâyân | doors |
| zânkoyân | universities |

The singular of the definite state of the noun is formed by adding **-aka** to the absolute form of the noun if it ends in a consonant or the vowels **u [w]**, **e**, and **i** and **-ka** after the vowels **o, a** and **â.** These endings are stressed.

|  |  |
|---|---|
| pyâwaka | the man |
| dergâka | the door |
| zânkoka | the university |

The plural of the definite state of the noun is formed by adding **-n** to the singular definite state of the noun.

|  |  |
|---|---|
| pyâwakân | the men |
| dergâkân | the doors |
| zânkokân | the universities |

These rules are best learned by repeating examples from the dialogs and from listening to the speech of native speakers.

## Examples

| | | |
|---|---|---|
| Şîr sipîye. | Milk is white. | شیر سپییه. |
| Şekir şîrîne. | Sugar is sweet. | شه کر شیرینه. |
| Hendê şâx le kurdistân zor berzin. | Some mountains in Kurdistan are very high. | هه ندئ شاخ له کوردستان زۆر به رزن. |
| zorbey kurdekân | most Kurds | زۆربه‌ی کورده‌کان |
| kitêb-i zor | a lot of books* | کتێبی زۆر |
| pyâwêk-i bâzâr | a man from the bazaar | پیاوێکی بازار |
| kogâyêk-i kem le bâzâr | a few stores in the bazaar | دوکانێکی که م له بازار |
| pyâweke le şârekewe. | the man from the city | پیاوه‌که له شاره‌که‌وه |
| zhinân le hewlêr | the women in Hewler | ژنان له هه‌ولێر |
| dukâneke-i nizîk bâxeke | the store near the park | دوکانه‌که‌ی نزیک باخه که |

*The idiom **-i zor,** "a lot of", always follows the indefinite singular of the noun. The construction [noun]-i [modifier] will be explained in Lesson 7.

Certain modifiers always take the indefinite singular in the following noun: **çend** "a few", **hemû** "every", **çi** "what", **her,** "each".

## Examples

çend zankoyek              a few universities
her pyâwek                  each man
hemû emêrikîek le a'êraq    every American in Iraq

## Words and phrases

| | |
|---|---|
| **şîr** | milk |
| **sipî** | white |
| **şekir** | sugar |
| **şîrîn** | sweet |
| **hendê** | some |
| **şâx/kêw** | mountain |
| **le kurdistân** | in Kurdistan |
| **zor** | very |
| **zorbey** | most |
| **gewre** | big |
| **kurd-i zor** | many Kurds |
| **kitêb** | book |
| **le bâzâr** | from the bazaar |
| **hemû emêrikîek** | every American |
| **a'êraq** | Iraq |
| **kogâyek-i kem** | few stores |
| **le şârekewe** | from the city |
| **nizîk** | near |
| **bâxeke** | the park |

**Translate into English.**

Ewâre bâş. Çonît?
Supâs. To bâşît?
Minîş bâşim, bellâm kemêk dwâdekewim.
Xwâ âgâdârit bê.
Farmû hendê âwî sârd.
Awe le Êrane.
Ame rêgâkeye bo bâxeke.
Awe bâxeke jwâne.

**Translate into Kurdish.**

Good evening. How are you?
I am well, thank you.
It is good to be here.
I am a little tired.
I must go.
Goodbye.

# Lesson 4 - The Restaurant

Gul and Dîlân have been shopping in the evening and have lost track of time. Gul notices the hour. She asks if Dîlân is hungry and interested in eating dinner at a restaurant. There are two good restaurants in the neighborhood, one Arabic and one Kurdish, and they decide to go to the Kurdish restaurant.

**Gul**

| | | |
|---|---|---|
| Dîlân, zor direnge. | Dilan, it is very late. | ديلان ، زۆر درەنگە. |
| Âya birsîte? | Are you hungry? | ئایە برسیتە؟ |
| Nizîkey sa'ât heşte | It is almost eight o'clock. | نزیکی سه عات هه شته. |

**Dîlân**

| | | |
|---|---|---|
| Bellê, zor birsîme. | Yes, I'm very hungry. | به لّی ، زۆر برسیمه. |
| Heşt! Pêm wâbû | Eight! I thought it | هەشت! پێم |

sa'ât <u>h</u>ewte. Êstâ
bâbiçîn nân
bixoîn.

was only seven.
Let's go eat now.

وا بوو سەعات
حەوتە. ئێستا
بابجين ، نان
بخۆين.

Âya çêşitxâne-i
bâşi lêye lem
nizîkâne ?

Is there a good
restaurant near
here?

ئایە چێشتخانەی
باشی لێیە لە م
نزیکانە؟

## Gul

Bellê.
Çêştixâneyekî
kurdî u a'erebî
lem nizîkâneye.

Yes. There is a
Kurdish and an
Arabic restaurant
near-by.

بە لّی
چێشتخانە یەکی
کوردی و
عەرەبی لەم
نزیکانەی

## Dîlân

Bâbiçîn bo
çêşitxâne
kurdîyeke.

Let's go to the
Kurdish
restaurant.

بابجين بۆ
چێشتخانە
کوردیەکە.

## Words and phrases

|  |  |
|---|---|
| **zor** | very |
| **direng** | late |
| **âya** | [introduces a question.] |
| **birsîte** | are you hungry? |
| **nizîki** | almost, nearly |
| **sa'ât** | hour |
| **bellê** | yes |
| **birsîme** | I am hungry |

33

| | |
|---|---|
| **heşt** | eight |
| **pêm wâbû** | I thought |
| **tenhâ** | only |
| <u>**h**</u>**ewt** | seven |
| **bâbiçîn** | let's go |
| **nân bixoîn** | let's eat [a meal] |
| **êstâ** | now |
| **çêşitxâne** | restaurant |
| **nizîk** | near |
| **lêye** | is there |
| **kurdî** | Kurdish |
| **u** | and |
| **a'erebî** | Arabic |
| **lem** | in, around |
| **bo** | to |
| **kurdîyeke** | the Kurdish |

## Verbs

The Kurdish verb system is extremely complex in comparison with that of English. For the beginner, it is sufficient to learn to speak simply in the present, future and past. Sorani has no separate future tense, and the present is used for the future in the same way as in English when we say "I am going now" and "I am going tomorrow." Later the past tense will be presented. There are other tenses, but learning the present, past, and future forms should suffice for the beginner.

## Endings for the present and future indictive

| If the verb stem ends in a consonant | | If the verb stem ends in a vowel | |
|---|---|---|---|
| I | -im | I | -m |
| you (sg.) | -î, ît | you (sg.) | -y, -yt |
| he/she/it | -ê or -êt | he/she/it | -â, -t, ât |
| we | în | we | -yn |
| you (pl.) | -in | you (pl.) | -n |
| they | -in | they | -n |

Present and future forms of the verb "to go" in the affirmative

| I go | deçim | we go | deçîn |
|---|---|---|---|
| you go (sg.) | deçît | you go(pl.) | deçin |
| he/she/it goes | deçê | they go | deçin |

## Examples

| Be nyâzim sibey biçme Hewlêr. | I am intending to go to Hewler (Erbil) tomorrow. | به نيازم سبه ى بچمه هه ولێر. |
|---|---|---|
| Âya Nîhâd legell ême dêt? | Will Nihad come with us? | ئايه نيهاد لهگهڵ ئێمه دێت؟ |
| Em pâse deçêt bo Silêmâni. | This bus goes to Sulaymaniye. | ئهم پاسه ده چێت بۆ سلێمانى؟ |
| Dwây nânî beyânî | After breakfast, I | دواى نانى به يانى، دهچم |

35

| deçim bo îş. | will go to work. | بۆ ئیش. |
| Âya rêgâ-i bâxeke dezânît? | Do you know the way to the park?. | ئایه رێگای باخەکە دەزانیت؟ |

## Words and phrases

| | |
|---|---|
| **nyâz** | need, intention |
| **sibey** | tomorrow |
| **çûn** | to go |
| **legell ême** | with us |
| **em pâse** | this bus |
| **dwây** | after |
| **nânî beyânî** | breakfast |
| **bo îş** | to work |
| **rêgâ-i bâxeke** | the way to the park |

## Translate into English.

Êwâre bâş. Zor direnge.
Bâbiçîn bo çêşitxâne kurdîyeke.
Qâwe yân çâ axoytewe?
Supâs, nâ. Kemêk mândûm.
Dâyikim ferensîye.
Boye be ferensî qise dekem.

## Translate into Kurdish.

My mother is French.
I only speak English.
I want to speak Kurdish.
My sister has two little girls.
I live with my husband.

Does he know the way to the restaurant?
Let's go to the park.

# Lesson 5 - Have You a Family?

At the restaurant, a traditional establishment, Gul and Dîlân seated in a screened off area where they are guarded from the looks of men who are in another part of the restaurant. Gul orders kebab and two glasses of juice. Then they discuss their families.

### Gul

| | | |
|---|---|---|
| Westâ, hezmân le dû şîş kebâbe. | Waiter, we would like two orders of kebab. | وەستا، حە زمان لە دوو شیش کە بابە. |
| Herwehâ, yek perdâx şerbet-i gêlas u yek perdâx şerbet-i pirteqâll. | Also, we would like a glass of cherry juice and a glass of orange juice. | هە روەها ، یەک پەرداخ شەربەتی گێلاس و یەک پەرداخ شە ر بەتی پرتەقا ڵ. |

### Gul

| | | |
|---|---|---|
| Pêm bille, âya xêzânît heye? | Tell me, do you have a family? | پێم بڵی ، ئایە خێزانیت هە یە؟ |

### Dîlân

| | | |
|---|---|---|
| Bellê. Legell bâwkim u dâykim u dû birâm dezhîm. | Yes. I live with my father and mother and two brothers. | بە ڵی ، لە گە ڵ باوکم و دایکم و دوو برام دەژیم. |

| | | |
|---|---|---|
| Herwehâ, xuşkêkim heya şwî kirdwe. Dû kiçî biçuk-i heye. | I also have a sister who is married. She has two little girls. | هه روهها، خوشکێکم هه یه که شوی کردوه، دوو کچی بچوکی هه یه. |

## Gul

| | | |
|---|---|---|
| Min legell hâwserekem u kurr- e biçuke çwâr sâllenekim dezhîm. | I live with my husband and my little boy. He is four. | من له گه لَ هاوسه‌ره‌که‌م وکوڕه بچوکه چوار سالآنه‌که‌م ده‌ژیم. |
| Ewe xwârdineke hât. a'âfêtân bê. | Here comes the food. Enjoy your meal. | ئه‌وه خواردنه‌که هات، عافیتان بێ. |

## Words and phrases

| | |
|---|---|
| **westâ** | polite word for "waiter" |
| **<u>h</u>ez** | like, desire |
| **le** | for |
| **dû** | two |
| **şîş** | shish |
| **kebab** | kebab |
| **herwehâ** | also |
| **yek** | one |
| **perdâx** | glass |
| **şerbet** | juice |
| **gêlas** | cherry |
| **pirteqâll** | orange |

39

| | |
|---|---|
| **pêm bille** | tell me |
| **xêzân** | family |
| **legell** | with |
| **bâwkim** | my father |
| **dâyîkim** | my mother |
| **birâm** | my brother |
| **dezhîm** | I live |
| **xuşkim** | my sister |
| **ke** | which |
| **şwî kirdwe** | married |
| **kiç** | girl, daughter |
| **biçuk** | little |
| **hâwserekem** | my husband |
| **kurr** | boy |
| **ew** | he |
| **sâll** | year (old) |
| **xwârdin** | food |
| **hât** | comes |
| **a'âfêtân** | *bon appetite* |

## Negative of the present and future indicative

To form the negative the prefix *de-* is replaced by the prefix *nâ-*.

Present tense of the verb "to go" in the negative

| | | | |
|---|---|---|---|
| I do not go | nâçim | we do not go | nâçîn |
| you not go (sg.) | nâçît | you do not(pl.) | nâçin |
| he/she/it does not go | nâçe | they do not go | nâçin |

## The verb "to know"

There are two words in Sorani for the English "to know":
*dezânim* and "I know", *denâsim*, "I am acquainted with".
*Dezânim* is used for knowledge of a factual nature: to
know something. *Denâsim* is used for acquaintanceship,
to know someone, be familiar with a city, etc.

## Examples

| | | |
|---|---|---|
| Em pâse nâçet bo şâreke. | This bus does not go to the city | ئه م پاسه ناچێت بۆ شارەکه؟ |
| Ew legell ême nâçet. | He is not going with us. | ئه و لهگهڵ ئێمه ناچێت؟ |
| Min kâk Âkâm nânâsim. | I do not know Kak Akam. | من كاك ئاكام نانــاسم. |
| Lêrewe çon detwânim biçim bo dukâneke ? | How do I go to the store from here? | لێرەوه ,چۆن ده توانم بچم بۆ دوکانهکه؟ |
| Bimbure. Nâzânim. | I'm sorry. I do not know. | بمبوره، نازانم. |

## Words and phrases

| | |
|---|---|
| **bo şârake** | to the city |
| **legell ême** | with us |
| **rêgâ-i bâxeke** | the way to the park |
| **nânâsim.** | I do not know |
| **lêrewe** | from here |

41

**Translate into English.**

1. Âya çêşitxâne-i bâşi lêye lem nizîkâne ?
2. Âya be kurdî qise dekeyt?
3. Be nyâzim sibey biçme Hewlêr.
4. Kogâyêk-i kem le bâzâr.
5. Hendê şâx le Kurdistân zor berzin.
6. Kemêk mândûm. Pewîste birrom.
7. Şew şâd. Xwâ âgâdârit bê.

**Translate into Kurdish.**

1. This bus goes to Sulaymaniye.
2. Does this bus go to Erbil?
3. I also have a sister.
4. My sister has a boy.
5. My brother has a boy.
6. She has a little boy who is two years old.
7. Tomorrow I must go to work.
8. My mother is French, so I speak French.
9. My mother speaks Kurdish.

# Lesson 6 - Where Is the Bazaar?

John has been wandering for almost an hour lost in the cold backstreets of a small city. Like many men, he does not like to ask directions, especially in a foreign language. He sees a local resident coming his way. He stops him, says he is lost and asks the way to the bazaar. The man tells him that it is quite some distance away and gives him directions.

## John

| | | |
|---|---|---|
| Çonî. Beyârmetît bâzâr lekwêye? | Hello. Excuse me, where is the bazaar? | چۆنی، بەیارمەتیت, بازار لە کوێیە؟ |

## The resident

| | | |
|---|---|---|
| Kemêk dûre. Dû kîlometir dûre. | It is a little far. It is two kilometers away. | کەمێک دوورە، دوو کیلۆ مه تر دوورە. |

43

## John

| | | |
|---|---|---|
| Lêrewe çon biçim? | How do I go from here? | لێرەوه ,چۆن بچم؟ |

## The resident

| | | |
|---|---|---|
| Bo lây rrâst biro bo bâxeke. | Go to the right to the park. | بۆ لای راست برۆ بۆ باخەکە. |
| Pêçkewe bo çep le bâxekewe, çwâr, pênj dukân debînî. | Turn left from the park, and you will see four or five shops | پێچ کەوە بۆ چەپ لە باخەکەوه، چوار، پێنج دوکان دەبینی. |
| Bâzâreke tenhâ sê xulek le dukânekânewe dûre. | The market is only three minutes from the shops. | بازارەکە تەنها سێ خولەک لە دوکانەکانەوه دووره. |

## John

| | | |
|---|---|---|
| Zor supâsit dekem. Xwâ âfîz. | Thank you very much. Goodbye. | زۆر سوپاست دەکەم، خواحافیز. |

## The resident

| | | |
|---|---|---|
| Şâyânî niye. Serçâwim. | You're welcome. Farewell. | شایانی نیه، سەرچاوم. |

## Words and phrases

| | |
|---|---|
| **çonî** | hello (how are you?) |
| **beyârmetît** | please, excuse me |
| **bâzâr** | bazaar, market |
| **lekwêye** | where is? |
| **kemêk** | a little |
| **dûr** | far |
| **dû** | two |
| **kîlometir** | kilometer |
| **min** | I |
| **lêrewe** | from here |
| **rrâst** | right |
| **biro** | go |
| **bo** | to |
| **pêçkewe** | turn around |
| **çep** | left |
| **bâxeke** | the park, garden |
| **çwâr** | four |
| **pênj** | five |
| **dukân** | store |
| **debînî** | you see |
| **bâzâreke** | the bazaar |
| **xulek** | minute |
| **le dukânekânewe** | from the stores |
| **supâsit dekem** | thank you |
| **şâyânî niye** | you are welcome |
| **niye** | is not |

## Cardinal numbers one to twelve

| | | | | | |
|---|---|---|---|---|---|
| 1 | yek | 5 | pênj | 9 | no |
| 2 | dû | 6 | şeş | 10 | de |
| 3 | sê | 7 | hewt | 11 | yâzde |
| 4 | çwâr | 8 | hêşt | 12 | dwâzde |

## "What time is it?" Kât çende?

Sorani normally operates with a twelve hour clock. The expression specifying the time of day may be added.

| | |
|---|---|
| morning | **serlebeyânî** |
| afternoon | **dwânîwerro** |
| evening | **êwâre** |
| night | **şew** |

The formula for expressing the hour is:
**sa'ât** + hour [+ **-i** + morning/afternoon/ evening/night]

To express minutes or quarter hour after the hour:
**sa'ât** + **hour** + **u** + minutes or quarter [**çârek**]

To express minutes or quarter hour before the hour:
**sa'ât** + minutes or quarter + **dewe bo** + hour

To express half past the hour:
**sa'ât** + hour + **u** + **nîwe**

## Examples

| | | |
|---|---|---|
| Beyârmetît. Kât çende? | Excuse me. What time is it? | به یارمەتیت، کات چەندە؟ |

| | | |
|---|---|---|
| Sa'ât de-i serlebeyânîye. | It is ten a.m.b | سەعات دە ی سەرلە بەانیە. |
| Sa'ât dû-i dwânîwerroye. | It is two in the afternoon. | سەعات دووی دوانیوەرۆیه. |
| Sa'at şeş-i êwâreye. | It is six in the evening | سەعات شەشی ئێوارهیه. |
| Sa'at de-i şewe. | It is ten at night. | سەعات دەی شه وه. |
| Sa'ât dû u nîwe | It is 2:30. | سەعات دوو ونیوه. |
| Sa'at pênj u de deqîqe. | It is 5:10. [5 and 10 minutes] | سەعات پێنج و ده دەقەیه. |
| Sa'ât çâregî dewê bo sê-i dwânîwerroye. | It is quarter to three p.m. | سەعات چارهگی دەوئ بۆ سئ دوا نیوەرۆ. |
| Sa'at no-i serlebeyânî dêm. | I am coming at nine a.m. | سەعات نۆی سه رلە بەیانی دێم. |

## The full form of the personal pronouns

Because the Sorani verb adds the enclitic or short form of the personal pronoun to the end of the verb, the full form is usually used only for emphasis or clarity.

| I | min | we | ême |
|---|---|---|---|
| you (sg.) | to | you (pl.) | êwe |

| he | ew | they (m.) | ewân |
| she | ew | they (f.) | ewân |
| it | ew | they (n.) | ewân |

**Examples**

| | |
|---|---|
| Min bâşim. | *I* am well. |
| Âya to kurdi? | Are *you* Kurdish? |

**Translate into English.**

1. Westâ, hezmân le dû şîş kebâbe
2. Supâs. Bâşe ke lêrey.
3. Bibure, âya be kurdî qise dekeyt?
4. Pêm billê, âya xêzânît heye?
5. Bâbiçîn nân bixoîn êstâ.
6. Sibey detbinmowe . Xwâ âfîz.
7. Nizîkey sa'ât hêşte.

**Translate into Kurdish.**

1. I was born in America.
2. You were botn in America.
3. My mother is French.
4. Are you American?
5. Do you speak French?
6. I must go now.
7. Where is the park?
8. How do I go from here?

## Lesson 7 – At the Clothing Store

Gul and Dîlân are out shopping. They decide to enter a clothing store. The brilliant colors of Kurdish women's clothing immediately catch their eyes. They spend some time in the store examining various items of clothing. The effect of color and contrast in the dresses is reminiscent of the saris of India. The women spend more than an hour looking at all of the clothing.

**Dîlân**

| | | |
|---|---|---|
| Âya ême detwânîn biçîn bo kogâyek-i jil u berig emrro? | Can we go to a clothing store today? | ئایه ئێمه دهتوانین بچین بۆ کۆگایهکی جل و بهرگ ئهمرۆ؟ |

**Gul**

| | | |
|---|---|---|
| Bedîllinyâyewe. Dû kogâ her lêren le tenîştîmânewe. | Certainly. There are two stores just here in the neighborhood. | به دڵنیایهوه دوو. کۆگا ههرلێرهن له ته نیشتمانهوه. |

| | | |
|---|---|---|
| Eme yekêkîâne. | Here is one. | ئە مە یە کێکیانە. |
| Bâ biçîne zhûrewe. | Let's go in. | بابچینە ژوورەوە. |

## Dîlân

| | | |
|---|---|---|
| Oy, jil u bergekân zor juânin. | Oh, the clothes are so beautiful. | ئۆی جلو بەرگەکان زۆر جوانن. |
| Jil u bergî kurdî zhinâne zor serinj-râkêşe. | Kurdish women's clothing is attractive. | جلوبەرگی کوردی ژنانە زۆر سەرنج راکێشە. |
| Âya ẖezit lem kirâse şîn u sipî heye? | Do you like this blue and white dress? | ئایە حەزت لەم کراسە شین و سپیە هەیە؟ |

## Gul

| | | |
|---|---|---|
| Ḫezdekem seyrî em kirâse xet, şîn u sur u rreşe bikem. | I would like to see that shirt with the blue, red and black stripes. | حەزدەکەم سەیری ئەم کراسە خەت ، شین و سور و رەشە بکەم. |
| Herwehâ ,em kirâse sewzeş juâne. | This green dress is also beautiful. | هەروەها,ئەم کراسە سەوزەش جوانە. |
| Nâtiwânim hellbizhêrim. | I just cannot choose. | ناتوانم هەڵبژێرم. |

50

## Words and phrases

| | |
|---|---|
| **detîwânîn** | we can |
| **çûn, (biçîn)** | go |
| **jil** | clothing |
| **berig** | clothing (and underwear) |
| **emrro** | today |
| **bedîllnyâyewe** | certainly |
| **tenîştîmânewe** | neighborhood |
| **yek** | one |
| **le nâu / zhûrewe** | in |
| **oy** | oh |
| **juân** | beautiful |
| **renge u reng** | colorful |
| **serinj-râkêş** | attractive |
| **hez** | desire |
| **hezdekem** | I would like |
| **kirâs** | dress |
| **şîn** | blue |
| **sipî** | white |
| **sur** | red |
| **rreş** | black |
| **xet** | stripe |
| **sewz** | green |
| **nâtiwânin** | cannot |
| **hellbizhârdin** | to choose |

## Pronoun endings indicating possession: "to have"

Personal pronouns may be added to nouns, to show to whom the noun belongs.

| my | nau**m** | my name |
| your (sg.) | nau**t** | your name |
| his/her/its | nau**y** | his/her/its name |
| our | nau**mân** | our name |
| your (pl.) | nau**tân** | your name |
| their | nau**yân** | their name |

In combination with the verb heye/niya, "there is", "there is not", this construction indicates possession.

| Çend pâret heye? | How much money do you have? |
| Kitêbim niye. | I have no books. |

## Modifiers - the *izâfa* construction

Adjectives and other modifiers in Kurdish follow the words they modify. The two elements are separated each other by the vowels *-i* or *-e*. This is known as the *izâfa* construction.

| kiçêk-i juân | a beautiful girl | کچێکی جوان |
| keş u hewâ-i xirâp | bad weather | که ش و هه وای خراپ |
| qutâbyân-i bâş | good students | قوتابیانی باش |

| | | |
|---|---|---|
| şârêk-i gewre | a large city | شارێکی گەورە |
| zhinêk-i uryâ | an intelligent woman | ژنێکی وریا |

This same construction is used to show possession as in the following examples:

| | | |
|---|---|---|
| zânko-i rrâperrîn | the University of Raparin | زانکۆی راپەرین |
| dergâ-i qutâbxâne | the door of the school | دەرگای قوتابخانە |
| pyâwân-i rânye | the men of Ranya | پیاوانی رانیە |
| berêweber-i bânqeke | the manager of the bank | بەرێوەبەری بانقە کە |
| dergâ-i qutâbxâne | the door of the school | دەرگای قوتابخانە |

With demonstrative adjectives and definite nouns, *e* substitutes for *i*.

| | | |
|---|---|---|
| pyâw-e bâşeke | the good man | پیاوە باشە کە |
| em pyâw-e bâşe | This man is good | ئەم پیاوە باشە |
| ew zhin-e juâne | That is a beautiful woman | ئەو ژنە جوانە |
| ew zhin-e juânâne | Those are beautiful women | ئەو ژنە جوانانە |

| | | |
|---|---|---|
| ew şâx-e gewrâne | those big mountains | ئەو شاخە گەورانە |
| ew kitêb-e qurse | that difficult book | ئەو کتێبە قورسە |
| ew qutâbxâne-i âmâdeye | that high school | ئەو قوتابخانەی ئامادەیە |
| ew qutâbxâne-i seretâî | those elementary schools | ئەو قوتابخانەی سەرەتای |
| ew qutâbyân-e le qutâbxâne-i âmâdeyn | these pupils from the high school | ئەو قوتابیانە لە قوتابخانەی ئامادەین |
| ew qutâbyân-e le zânkoy rrâparrînin | those students from Raparin university | ئەو قوتابیانە لە زانکۆی راپەرینن |
| xânû-e şîneke | the blue house | خانووە شینەکە |
| hewr-e rreşeke | the gray cloud | هەورە رەشە کە |

## Words and phrases

| | |
|---|---|
| **keş u hewâ** | weather |
| **xirâp** | bad |
| **qutâbyân** | students |
| **dâr** | tree |
| **şâr** | city |
| **zhin** | woman |
| **uryâ** | intelligent |
| **xânû** | house |
| **bînâ** | building |
| **krâse** | dress |

| | |
|---|---|
| **hewr** | cloud |
| **rreş** | black (dark) |
| **şâx** | mountain |
| **gewre** | big |
| **kitêb** | book |
| **quris** | difficult |
| **qutâbxânekân** | schools |
| **qutâbxâne-i seretâî** | elementary school |
| **qutâbxâne-i âmâdeyken** | high schools |

## Translate into English.

Westâ, hezmân le dû şîş kebâbe.
Herwehâ, yek perdâx şerbetî gelâs.
Pêm billê, âya xêzânît heye?
Bellê . Legell bukim u dâyîkim u dû birâm dezhîm.
Min legell hâwserekem u kurr-e biçukekem dezhîm
Bâzâreke tenhâ se xulek le dukânekenewe dûre.

## Translate into Kurdish.

Do you like this book?
Do you like the restaurant?
The beautiful woman is my sister.
The woman is my mother.
This is the way to the university.
That is the way to the park.
The red shirt is beautiful.
The mountains in Kurdistan are very high.

# Lesson 8 – At the Pharmacy

John is walking with a friend through the bazaar. He has been suffering from a headache and wants to buy a pain reliever. Many medicines are available without prescription. He speaks with the druggist, and after he receives the medicine, he asks if there is a doctor in the neighborhood. The druggist replies that there is a doctor's office across the street and that there is also a hospital nearby.

## John

| | | |
|---|---|---|
| Âyâ ême detwânîn lew dermânxâneye biwestîn lewê? | Could we stop at the pharmacy over there? | ئایه ئێمه ده توانین له و دەرمانخانهیه بوەستین له وئ؟ |

## Druggist

| | | |
|---|---|---|
| Beyânî bâş. Çon detwânim yârmetît bidem? | Good morning. How may I help you? | بەیانی باش، چۆن ده توانم یارمه تیت بدەم؟ |

56

## John

| | | |
|---|---|---|
| Hezdekem hendê şit bikirrim bo ser eşe. | I would like to buy something for a headache. | حه‌ زده‌ كه‌م هه‌ندئ شت بكرم بۆ سه‌رئێشه. |
| Detwânî pêşniyâr-i diktorêkîş bikeyt? | Can you also recommend a doctor? | ده‌توانى پێشنیارى دكتۆرێكیش بكه‌یت؟ |

## Druggist

| | | |
|---|---|---|
| Diktor Ârâm Xizir Aḥmed nusîngeke-i lewberî şeqâmekeweye. | Dr. Aram Khazir Ahmed has his office across the street. | دكتۆر ئارام خزر ئه‌ حمه‌ د نوسینگه‌كه‌ى له‌وبه‌رى شه‌قامه‌كه‌ وه‌یه. |
| Herwehâ lem nizîkâne nexoşxâneyek heye. | There is also a hospital near-by. | هه‌روه‌ها له‌ م نزیكانه. نه‌خۆشخانه‌یه‌ك هه‌یه. |

## John

| | | |
|---|---|---|
| Zor supâsit dekem. | Thank you very much. | زۆر سوپاست ده‌كه‌م. |

## Words and phrases

| | |
|---|---|
| **dermânxâne** | pharmacy |
| **westân** | stop |
| **lewê** | there |
| **çon** | how |

57

| | |
|---|---|
| **yârmetît bidem** | help (you) |
| **hezdekem** | would like |
| **hendê şit** | something |
| **bikirrim** | I may buy |
| **sereşe** | headache |
| **detwânî** | can you |
| **diktor** | doctor |
| **îş** | also (at end of a noun) |
| **pêşniyâr kirdin** | recommend |
| **nusînge** | office |
| **lewberî** | across |
| **şeqâm** | street |
| **nizîkâne** | neighborhood |
| **nexoşxâne** | hospital |
| **supâs bo to** | thanks to you |
| **dedem** | I give |

## Comparative and superlative of adjectives

To form the comparative of an adjective, simply add **-tir**.
Example: "good", **bâş**; "better", **bâştir**.
To form the superlative, add **-tirîn**. Example: "best",
**bâştirîn**.

These changes are regular for all adjectives

## Examples

| | | |
|---|---|---|
| bâştirîn kitêb | the best book | باشترین کتێب |
| rêgâyek-i bâştir | a better road | ڕێگایەکی باشتر |
| direzhtirîn rrozh | the longest day | درێژترین ڕۆژ |
| şâxêk-i gewretir | a bigger mountain | شاخێکی گەورەتر |
| bâştirîn zânko | the best university | باشترین زانکۆ |
| xiraptirîn syâsetmedâr | the worst politician | خراپترین سیاسەتمەدار |
| gemzhetirîn serbâz | the stupidest soldier | گە مژە ترین سەرباز |
| zîrektirîn qutâbî | the smartest student | زیرەکترین قوتابی |
| zeyneb şoxtire le şlêr | Zeyneb is prettier than Shler | زەینەب شۆختره لە شلێر |

## The verb "to come", hâtin

Present tense of the irregular verb "to come" in the affirmative

| | | | |
|---|---|---|---|
| I come | dêm | we come | dêyn |
| you come (sg.) | dêyt | you come (pl.) | dên |
| he/she/it comes | dê | they come | dên |

Present tense of the irregular verb "to come" in the negative

| I do not come | nâyem | we do not come | nâyeyn |
| you not come (sg.) | nâyeyt | you do not come (pl.) | nâyen |
| he/she/it does not come | nâye | they do not come | nâyen |

## Words and phrases

| | |
|---|---|
| **direzh** | long |
| **rrozh** | day |
| **syâsetmedâr** | politician |
| **gemzhetirîn** | stupidest |
| **serbâz** | soldier |
| **zîrektirîn** | smartest |
| **şoxtir** | prettier |

## Translate into English.

Bâxêrbêy. Tikâye were zhûrewe.

Supâs, diktor Âzâd. Bâşe ke lêrey.

Âya birsîte? Nizîkey sa'ât hêşte

Âya çêşitxâne-i bâş lem nizîkâne heye?

Nîwerro bâş.

Bibure, âya be kurdî qise dekeyt?

Detwânim kemêk be kurdî qise bikem, bellâm be
    tewawî nâ.

**Translate into Kurdish.**

Where is the bazaar?
Where is the store.
What time is it?
It is three in the afternoon.
It is seven in the evening.
A better book
A good university

**Barzan hospital in Dohuk**

# Lesson 9 – Erbil (Arbil, Hewler)

Sarkawt has driven his friend John to see the capital of the Iraqi Kurdistan Region. The name of the city is a bit confusing because it is sometimes called Erbil or Arbil, the Arabic name for the city. The Kurdish name is Hewler. All three names are in use. John marvels at the modernity of the city with its broad roads and tall buildings. At the center of the city is the Citadel, reputedly the oldest urban settlement in the world. It is now the site of a ruined Ottoman fortress.

## Sarkawt

| | | |
|---|---|---|
| Ême degayne hewlêr, pâytext-i herêm-i kurdîstân. | We are arriving at Hewler, the capital of the Kurdistan Region. | ئێمه ده‌ گه‌ ینه‌ هه‌ ولێر پایته‌ختی هه‌رێمی کوردستان . |

**John**

| Çî şitêk lêrewe debînîrêt? | What is there to be seen here? | چی شتێک لێرەوه دە بینیرێت؟ |

**Sarkawt**

| Bêgumân, bînâ <u>h</u>ukumiakân heye. | Of course, there are the government buildings. | بێ گومان بینا حکومیەکان هەیه. |
| Giringtirîn şwên sîtâdêle. | The most important place is the citadel. | گرنگترین شوێن سیتادێله. |

**John**

| Sîtâdêl çîye? | What is the citadel? | سیتادێل ، چی یه؟ |

**Sarkawt**

| Wâtâ qellâ. | It means fort. | واتا قه لا. |

**John**

| Zorbey şâreke zor nwê dête pêş çâw. | Most of the city seems very new. | زۆربەی شارەکه زۆر نوێ دێته پێش چاو. |

## Sarkawt

| | | |
|---|---|---|
| Bellê. Bînâ serdemyekân u rêgâkân tâzen. | Yes, the modern buildings and roads are new. | به لّی بینا سەردەمیەکان و ڕێگاکان تازەن. |
| Bellâm ême kêşe-i xirâpî tirâfîkalâîtmân zore. | But we do have a very bad traffic problem. | بەلّام ئێمه کێشەی خراپی ترافیکلایتمان زۆره. |
| Seyâre-i zorî lêye. | There are too many cars. | سەیارەی زۆری لێیه. |

## Words and phrases

| | |
|---|---|
| **geyştin, ge-** | to arrive |
| **pâytext** | capital |
| **herêm** | region |
| **şit** | thing |
| **bînîn** | to see |
| **bê gumân** | of course |
| **bînâkân** | the buildings |
| **ḥukumet** | government |
| **giringtirîn** | most important |
| **şiwên** | place |
| **sîtâdêl** | citadel |
| **çîye** | what is? |
| **wâtâ** | it means |
| **qellâ** | fort |
| **zorbey** | most |
| **şâreke** | the city |

| | |
|---:|:---|
| **nwê** | new |
| **dân** | give |
| **pêş** | in front |
| **çâw** | eye |
| **dête pêş çâw** | to seem |
| **serdemyene** | modern |
| **rêgêkên** | roads |
| **tâze** | new |
| **kêşe** | problem |
| **xirâp** | bad |
| **tirâfîkalâît** | traffic |
| **otombîl, seyâre** | car |
| **lêye** | there are, there is |

## The Subjunctive

Sorani verbs have both an indicative form (describing what is actually the case) and a subjunctive form (describing what might or should be the case). We have already met the subjunctive forms of verbs in the dialogs. In Kurdish the subjunctive is widely used, often as the second verb after an expression of desire, possibility or intention. Do not be disturbed if you find slight variations in the forms: e.g., the addition of a *-t* to third person forms.

## Examples from the dialogs:

| | |
|:---|:---|
| Ême detwânîn lew dermânxâne *biwestîn* | Can we stop in a pharmacy? |
| Hezdekem hendê şit | I want to buy |

65

| *bikirrim.* | something. |
| --- | --- |
| Detwânî diktorêkeş pêşniyâr *bikeyt?* | Can you also recommend a doctor? |

In the subjunctive affirmative, the prefix **da-** is replaced by **bi-**. In the negative **da-** is replaced by **nâ-**.

Present subjunctive forms of the verb "to go"

| affirmative | | negative | |
| --- | --- | --- | --- |
| I go | biçim | I do not go | nâçim |
| you go (sg.) | biçît | you do not go (sg.) | nâçît |
| he/she/it goes | biçê | he/she/it does not go | nâçê |
| we go | biçîn | we do not go | nâçîn |
| you go (pl.) | biçin | you do not go (pl.) | nâçin |
| they go | biçin | they do not go | nâçin |

Simple subjunctive form of the verb "to be"

| I am | bim | we are | bîn |
| --- | --- | --- | --- |
| you are (sg.) | bît | you are (pl.) | bin |
| he/she/it is | bê | they are | bin |

The alternative form of the verb "to be" with the prefix *bi-* often has the connotation of becoming.

| I become | bibim | we become | bibîn |
| --- | --- | --- | --- |
| you become (sg.) | bibît | you become (pl.) | bibin |
| he/she/it becomes | bibê | they become | bibin |

The subjunctive expresses desire, potential, or cases contrary to fact. The subjunctive is always used whenever a verb follows the verb "to want", **wîstin.**

The irregular present affirmative of "to want":

| | | | |
|---|---|---|---|
| I want | demewe | we want | demânewe |
| you want (sg.) | detewe | you want (pl.) | detânewe |
| he/she/it wants | deyewe | they want | deyânewe |

Note:: -ewe ending may be ewê in some dialects.

Present negative of the verb "to want"

| | | | |
|---|---|---|---|
| I do not want | namewê | we do not want | namânewê |
| you do not want (sg.) | natewê | you do not want (pl.) | natânewê |
| he/she/it does not want | nayewê | they do not want | nayânewê |

## Examples

| | | |
|---|---|---|
| Dey bâbiçîn bo kogâke. | Let's go to the store. | دەی بابچین بۆ کۆگاکه. |
| Ew deyewêt kitêbeket bibînê. | He wants to see your book. | ئه و ده یه وێت کتێبه کهت ببینێ. |
| Ew deyewêt biçet bo çêştixâne kurdîyeke. | She wants to go to the Kurdish restaurant. | ئه و ده یه وێت بچێت بۆ چێشتخانه کوردیهکه. |
| Ewân deyânewêt | They want to | ئه وان |

67

| zânkoke bidozinewê. | find the university. | ده يانهوێت زانکۆکه بدۆزنهوه. |
| A'lî nâyewê qise bikat. | Ali does not want to talk. | على نايهوئ قسه بکات. |
| Min demewê Slêmânî bibînim. | I want to see Sulaymaniye. | من ده مهوئ سلێمانى ببينم. |

## Words and phrases

| **bâbçin** | let's go |
| **deyewêt bibînê** | wants to see |
| **deyewêt biçêt** | wants to go |
| **dozinewe** | to find |
| **nayewê** | does not want |
| **qise bikat** | to talk |
| **demewê bibinim** | I want to see |

## Translate into English.

Pêm billê, âya xêzânît heye?
Min legell hâwserekem u kurr-e biçukekem dezhîm.
Herwehâ xuşkim heye şwî kirdwe.
Çon detwânim yârmetit bidem?
Âya hezit lem kirâse şîn u sipye heye?
Em kirâse sewzeş jwâne.
Em pâse deçêt bo Slêmânî.
Westâ, hezmân le dû şîş kebâbe.

**Translate into Kurdish.**

Would you like tea?
Shall we go to the restaurant?
Shall we go to the park?
Is he going to the park?
Are you going to the restaurant?
Good evening, Sarkawt. How are you?
My sister does not want to come.
My father does not want to go.
I want to go to the store.
Is this the way to the bazaar?
I want to go to the bazaar.
Do you want to go to the restaurant?

| 0 | 1 | 2 | 3 | 4 |
|---|---|---|---|---|
| ٠ | ١ | ٢ | ٣ | ٤ |
| 5 | 6 | 7 | 8 | 9 |
| ٥ | ٦ | ٧ | ٨ | ٩ |

**For those of you who want to read license plates in northern Iraq**

# Lesson 10 - The Anfal Monument

**Memorial to the victims of the Anfal massacre of
the Kurds by Saddam Hussein in 1986 -1988**

As John and Sarkawt drive out of Erbil on a road
that leads through a valley, they pass a huge monument
on a hill to the right. John asks what it is, and Sarkawt
explains that it was built in memory of the victims of the
Anfal, the genocidal attack on the Kurdish people by
Saddam Hussein. In 1988 he tried to remove or destroy
all Kurds living in this part of Iraq. In 2003 the Kurds
took advantage of the American invasion of the country
to establish a government and military that is semi-
independent of Baghdad and which carries on economic
and diplomatic relations with foreign governments.

## John

| | | |
|---|---|---|
| Em peykere | What is that | ئەم پەیکەرە |
| bîrewerye gewre | huge statue | بیرەوەریە گەورە |
| çîye ke le ser em | monument on | چی یە کە لە سەر |
| girdeye lewê? | the hill over | ئەم گردەیە |
| | there? | لە وێ؟ |

## Sarkawt

Ewe bo qurbânyân-i enfâle.

That is to the victims of the Anfal.

ئەوە بۆ قوربانیانی ئەنفاله.

Enfâl cînosâyd bû dizhî Kurdekân le 1988.

The Anfal was the genocide against the Kurds in 1988.

ئە نفال جینۆ ساید بوو دژی کوردەکان لە ۱۹۸۸.

Dwây 2003 nâwçe-i kurdî dast pêkird be dirustikirdinî herêmêk-i jyâ kirâwe le a'êrâq.

After 2003 the Kurdish area began to build a separate region in Iraq.

دوای ۲۰۰۳ ناوچەی کوردی دەستی پێکرد بە دروست کردنی هەرێمێکی جیا کراوه لە عێراق.

Herêmeke-i ême hêzêk-i gewre-i serbâz-i nâsirâw be pêşmergey heye.

Our region keeps a large army known as the Peshmerga.

هەرێمە کەی ئێمە هێزێکینی گەورەی سە ربازی ناسراو بە پێشمەرگەی هەیه.

## John

Wâtây pêşmerge çîye?

What does Peshmerga mean?

واتای پێشمەرگه چی یه؟

### Sarkawt

Wâtâ "awâne-i rûyân le merge".

It means "those who face death".

واتا، ئەوانەى روويان لە مەرگە.

### Words and phrases

| | |
|---|---|
| peyker | statue |
| bîrewerye | monument |
| le ser | on |
| gird | hill |
| gewre | large |
| bo qurbânyekân | to the victims |
| enfâle | Anfal |
| cînosâyd | genocide |
| dizh | against |
| nâwçe | area |
| dast + pêkirdin | to begin |
| dirustikirdin | to build |
| herêm | territory |
| jyâ | separate, independent |

| | |
|---|---|
| **kirâwe** | open |
| **hêz** | army, force |
| **serbâz** | soldier |
| **nâsirâw** | known |
| **weku** | like, as |
| **pêşmerge** | Peshmerga |
| **wâtâ** | means |
| **awâne** | those |
| **rûxsâr** | face |
| **mirdin, merg** | death |

## The verb *twânîn*, "to be able"

Twânîn is always followed by the subjunctive.
Present affirmative: "to be able to go"

| | |
|---|---|
| detwânîm biçim | I am able to go |
| detwânît biçît | you (sg.) are able to go |
| detwânê biçê | he/she/it is able to go |
| detwânîn biçîn | we are able to go |
| detwânin biçin | you (pl.) are able to go |
| detwânin biçin | they are able to go |

Present negative: "not to be able to go"

| | |
|---|---|
| natwânîm biçim | I am not able to go |
| natwânît biçît | you (sg.) are not able to go |
| natwânê biçê | he/she/it is not able to go |
| natwânîn biçîn | we are not able to go |
| natwânin biçin | you (pl.) are not able to go |
| natwânin biçin | they are not able to go |

**Translate into English.**

Çon biçim lêrewe?
Pêçkewe bo çep le bâxekewe.
Bâzâreke tenhâ se xulek dûre.
Pewîste êstâ birrom.
Min beyânî to debînmewe. Xwâ âfîz.
Bibure hendê âwî sârd.
Qâwe yân çâ axoytewe ?
Bibure, âya be kurdî qise dekeyt?

**Translate into Kurdish.**

I am a little tired. I should go.
Where are you from?
Are you American?
Does your little girl speak French?
I do not speak enough Kurdish.
I cannot go to the park.
I cannot see your book.

# Lesson 11 - Mountains and Valleys

John is impressed by the beauty of the mountainous area outside of Hewler. He asks Sarkawt if it is possible to drive into the mountains and valleys. The fact that driving conditions can be challenging or even dangerous leads Sarkawt to insist that they find an expert driver in order to take this trip. They find a driver and set out on the road to the countryside. The countryside in the spring is extremely beautiful, and they decide to stop and have a picnic.

## John

| | | |
|---|---|---|
| Deşt u der-i dewru berî hewlêr zor jwâne. | The countryside around Erbil is very beautiful. | دەشت و دەری دەورو بەری هەولێر زۆر جوانە. |
| Detwânîn biçîn be otombîl lêxûrrin? | Can we go for a drive? | دەتوانین بچین بە ئۆتۆمۆبیل لێخوورین؟ |

## Sarkawt

| | | |
|---|---|---|
| Yekemjâr pêwîste şufêrêkî bâş bıdozînewe. | First we must find a good driver. | یه‌ که‌ م جار پێویسته‌ شۆفێرێکی باش بدۆزینه‌وه‌. |
| Rêgâkân betewâwetî selâmet nîn. | The roads are not completely safe. | رێگاکان به‌ ته‌واوه‌تی سه‌لامه‌ت نین. |
| Le nêwan rêgây êre u Rânye, beşêk qîrnekirâw heye. | On the road between here and Ranya, there is an unpaved section. | له‌ نێوان رێگای ئێره‌ و رانیه‌ ، به‌شێک قیرنه‌کراو هه‌یه‌. |
| Bemduwâyâne em rêgâyey ser şaxeke dirust kirâwe. | Recently this road was built over the mountain. | به‌ م دوایانه‌ ، ئه‌م رێگایه‌ی سه‌ر شاخه‌که‌ دروست کراوه‌. |
| Le serewe detwânîn dolekân, lâdêkân, u deştekân bibînîn. | From the top we can see valleys, villages and fields. | له‌ سه‌ره‌وه‌ ده‌توانین دۆله‌کان لادێکانو ده‌شته‌کان ببینین. |
| Le behârdâ zew-i sewz debêt be çendehâ gul-i siruştî. | In the spring the land is green with many wildflowers. | له‌ به‌ هاردا زه‌وی سه‌وز ده‌بێت به‌ چه‌نده‌ها گولی سروشتی. |

## John

| | | |
|---|---|---|
| Bâ lenizîk ew rûbâre lexwâr ewê buwestîn u seyrânêk rêkbıxeyn | Let's stop by that river down there and have a picnic. | با له نزیک ئهو رووباره له خوار ه وه بوهستین و سهیرانێک رێکبخه ین. |

## Words and phrases

| | |
|---|---|
| **deşt u der** | countryside |
| **dewru berî** | around |
| **seyâre lêxûrrin** | to go for a drive |
| **yekem jâr** | first |
| **şofêr** | driver |
| **dozînewe** | find |
| **rêgâkân** | roads |
| **betewâwetî** | completely |
| **selâmet** | safe |
| **nêwan** | between, among |
| **beş** | part, section |
| **qîrkirâw** | paved |
| **ser** | head, top |
| **şâxeke** | the mountain |
| **dirustikirdin** | build |
| **bemduwâyâne** | recently |
| **le ser** | on top of |
| **dolekân** | valleys |
| **lâdêkân** | villages |
| **deştekân** | fields |
| **le  bahârdâ** | in spring |

77

| | |
|---|---|
| **zewî** | land |
| **sewz** | green |
| **debêt** | is (becomes) |
| **çendehâ** | many |
| **gul** | flower |
| **siruştî** | wild |
| **rubâreke** | the river |
| **westân** | stop |
| **xwârewe** | down |
| **seyrân** | picnic |
| **rêkxistin** | to arrange |

## Prepositions and "circumpositions"

Prepositions precede the word they modify, as in English.

"with", **legell**
"without", **bê**
"to", **bo**
"in", **le nâw**  "from", **le**
"on" or "on top of", **le ser**
"after", **pâş**
"before", **peş**
"through", **benâw**

Circumpositions come before the word modified, but add the endings **-awe**, **-â** or **-de** at the end: **legell minâ**, "with me"; **le kurdistânâ**, "in Kurdistan".

## Examples

| | | |
|---|---|---|
| le  hewlêr | from Hewler (Erbil) | له هه و لێر |

| | | |
|---|---|---|
| le dwây mizgewt | after the mosque | له دوای مزگەوت |
| le ser şâx | on the mountain | له سه ر شاخ |
| legell daykim | with my mother | له گەڵ دایکم |
| Be zânko dellên çî be kurdi? | how do you say "university" in Kurdish? | به زانکۆ ده لّێن چی به کوردی؟ . |
| pêş no-i êware | before 9 pm | پێش نۆی ئێواره |
| dwây dû şemme | after Monday | دوای دوو شەممه |
| benâw şârekedâ | through the city | بەناو شارەکەدا |

## Translate into English.

Bibure, âya be kurdî qise dekeyt?
Le kwewe hâtwî?
Min le emirîkâ le dâyk bûm.
Dâyîkim ferensîye. Boye be ferensî qise dekem.
Detwânî pêşnıyâr- i diktorêkîş bikeyt?
Âya çêşitxâne-i bâş lem nizîkâne heya?
Bellê. Çêştixâneyek-i kurdî u a'erebî lem nizîkâneye.

## Translate into Kurdish.

My sister is in the park.
This university is on a mountain.
You cannot go to Hewler.
We can go on the bus to Sulaymaniye.
I live with my brothers and sisters.
Let's go to the French restaurant.
We can go to the village.
Do you want to have a picnic by the river?

# Lesson 12 – A Village

Many Kurds live in remote mountain villages, some of which seem untouched by modern development. The Kurdistan Regional Government has made progress in bringing electricity, sanitation, and rudimentary health care to many communities, but some of them exist in virtual isolation, living off agriculture and their animals. John has gone with a couple of Kurdish friends on a trek through the mountains and spent some time in one such village. He describes it to a friend.

## John

| | | |
|---|---|---|
| Şemmey râbîrdû ême çûyn bo gundêk-i biçuk le şâxekân. | Last Saturday we went to a small village in the mountains. | شەممەی رابردوو ئێمە چووین بۆ گوندێکی بچوک لە شاخەکان. |

## Martin

| | | |
|---|---|---|
| Çon bû? We çend xellkî lê dezhyâ? | What was it like? How many people lived there? | چۆن بوو؟ وە چەند خەڵکی لێ دەژیا؟ |

80

## John

Lewâneye nizîkey bîst xêzânêk hebin lewê.

There may have been about twenty families.

لەوانەیە نزیکەی بیست خێزانێک هەبن لە وێ.

Emâne çutyârî isâdebûn ke merr u biznyân be xêwdekird.

These were simple farmers tending sheep and goats.

ئەمانە جوتیاری ساده بوون که مەڕو بزنیان به خێودەکرد.

## Martin

Dâb u nerîtekân çon bûn lewê?

What were the conditions like?

دابوو نه ریتەکان چۆن بوون لە وێ؟

## John

Xellk êmey de'awet kird bo çâ.

People invited us in for tea.

خەڵک ئێمەی دەعوەت کرد بۆ چا

Xânwekân sâdebûn bellâm zor xâwên bûn.

The houses were simple but very clean.

خانوەکان ساده بوون به لام زۆر خاوێن بوون.

Herçende lâdêke dûr bû le şâreka, kârebây hebû.

Even though the village was far from the city, there was electricity.

هەرچەندە لادێکه دوور بوو لە شارەکه ، کارەبای هه بوو.

81

| | | |
|---|---|---|
| Le êwâredâ xêzânekân beyeke seyrî televizyonyân kird. | In the evening families watched television together. | له ئێوارەدا، خێزانه کان بەیەکەوه سەیری تەلەفزیونیان کرد. |

## Words and phrases

| | |
|---|---|
| şemme | Saturday |
| râbîrdû | past |
| çûyn | we went |
| gund | village |
| çon bû | what was it like? |
| zhyân (zhî-) | to live |
| zhimâre | number |
| bîst | twenty |
| xêzân | family |
| hebîn | to have been |
| çutyâr | farmer |
| sâde | simple |
| merr | sheep |
| bizin | goat |
| bexêwkîrdin | to tend |
| dâb u nerîtekân | condition |
| de'awet kirdin | to invite |
| xânû | house |
| xâwên | clean |
| herçende | even though |
| lâdê | village |
| kârebâ | electricity |

82

| | |
|---|---|
| **lêbû** | there was |
| **le êwâredâ** | in the evening |
| **beyekewe** | together |
| **seyrî kirdin** | to watch |

## The infinitive and the formation of the simple past tense

The infinitive in Sorani is the form of the verb which is listed in the dictionary, in the same way that the absolute state of the noun is the form listed in the dictionary.

The past tense is formed by dropping the **-n** from the infinitive and adding the following endings to the stem of the verb:

| If the verb stem ends in a consonant | | If the verb stem ends in a vowel | |
|---|---|---|---|
| -im | -în | -m | -yn |
| -ît | -in | -yt | -n |
| - | -in | - | -n |

**Examples:** *nusin*, "to write", *çûn*, "to go".

| | | | |
|---|---|---|---|
| I wrote | nusim | I went | çûm |
| you (sg.)wrote | nusît | you (sg.) went | çûyt |
| he/she/it wrote | nusi | he/she/it went | çû |
| we wrote | nusîn | we went | çûyn |
| you (pl.) wrote | nusin | you (pl.) went | çûn |
| they wrote | nusin | they went | çûn |

The negative is formed by adding the stressed prefix *na-* to the simple past: *nahâtim,* "I did not come"; *nabûm,* I was not.

## Translate into English.

Zorbey şâreke zor nwê dête pêş çâw.

Bellê. Bînâ serdemyekân u rêgêkên tâzen.

Bellâm seyâre-i zorî lêye.

Dwây 2003 nâwçe-i kurdî destî kird be dirustikirdîny herêmêk-i jyâ kirâwe le a'êrâq.

Herêmekey ême hêzêk-i gewrey serbâzî nâsirâw be pêşmergi heye.

Âyâ ême detwânîn le dermânxâne biwestîn lewê?

Hezdekem hendê şit bikirim bo sereşe.

Detwânî peşniyârî diktorêkîş bikeyt?

## Translate into Kurdish.

The road is not safe.

Erbil is very far from here.

Can you help me speak Kurdish?

Let us go get tea.

The restaurant is not very far away.

It is ten at night. Let's go.

I wrote a book.

He came from Erbil.

We went to Dohuk.

They saw the village on the mountain.

# Lesson 13 – Qaladze

From 1986 until 1988, Saddam Hussein waged a genocidal compaign, the Anfal, which targeted the Kurds. Thousands of Kurdish villages were destroyed. Perhaps the best known atrocity was the gas attack on the city of Halajba, which killed about 5000 civilians. Qaladze was one of the cities and towns destroyed by aerial bombardment. At that time there was a campus of Sulaymaniye University in the town. It was targeted by the Iraqi air force, and hundreds of students and teachers were killed. Millions of Kurds from the region fled into the mountains with their donkeys.

## Sarkawt

| | | |
|---|---|---|
| Her êstâ ême le nizîk Qellâdzê-i lêdexurîn. | Right now we are driving near Qaladze. | ھەر ئێستا ئێمە لە نزیک قەلادزی لێده خورین. |

| | | |
|---|---|---|
| Le mâwe-i rreşekuzhyekedâ lêre Sedâm zânkoy bordumân kirdi. | During the genocide Saddam bombed the university. | له ماوهی رهشهکوژیهکهدا لێره, سهدام زانکۆی بۆردومان کرد. |
| Hewlîdâ hemû Kurdekân bigwâzêtewe le nâwçekedâ. | He tried to move all of the Kurds out of this area. | ههولێدا ههموو کوردهکان بگوازیتهوه له ناوچهکه دا. |
| Dû milyon Kurd be kerekânyân hellâtin bo şâxekân. | Two million Kurds fled with their donkeys into the mountains. | دوو ملیۆن کورد به کهرهکانیان ههڵاتن بۆ شا خه کان. |
| Hendêjâr Kurdekân dellên tâke hâwrêyân le jîhândâ şâxekânin. | Sometimes Kurds say that their only friends in the world are the mountains. | هه ندێجار کوردهکان ده لێن تاکه هاوڕێیان له جیهاندا شاخهکانین. |
| Bellâm êstâ nişâne-i pêşkewtin u geşekirdin bedî dekrêt. | But now there are signs of development and progress here. | بهڵام ئیستا نیشانهی پێشکهوتن و گه شهکردن به دی ده کرێت. |

**Words and phrases**

|  |  |
|---|---|
| **her êstâ** | right now |
| **lêdexurîn** | we are driving |

86

| | |
|---:|:---|
| **le mâwe-i** | during |
| **rreşekuzhî** | the genocide |
| **hewlîdân** | try |
| **gwâstinewe, gwez-ewe** | remove, move out |
| **hellâtin** | flee |
| **ker** | donkey |
| **hendêçâr** | sometime |
| **dellên** | they say |
| **hâwrrî** | friend |
| **take, tenhâ** | only |
| **jîhân** | world |
| **nişâneken** | signs |
| **pêşkewtin** | progress |
| **geşekirdin** | development |
| **bedî dekrêt** | there are |

## The past tense forms of "to be" and "to have"

The past form of the verb "to be" in the affirmative

| I was | bûm | we were | bûyn |
|---|---|---|---|
| you were (sg.) | bûy | you were(pl.) | bûn |
| he/she/it was | bû | they were | bûn |

The past form of the verb "to be" in the negative

| I was not | nebûm | we were not | nebûyn |
|---|---|---|---|
| you were not (sg.) | nebûy | you were not (pl.) | nebûn |
| he/she/it was not | nebû | they were not | nebûn |

The past form of the verb "to have" in the affirmative

| I had | hem bû | we had | hemân bû |
|---|---|---|---|
| you had (sg.) | het bû | you had (pl.) | hetân bû |
| he/she/it had | hey bû | they had | heyân bû |

The past form of the verb "to have" in the negative

| I did not have | nem bû | we did not have | nemân bû |
|---|---|---|---|
| you did not have (sg.) | net bû | you did not have (pl.) | netân bû |
| he/she/it did not have | ney bû | they did not have | neyân bû |

## Examples

| Mâmostâkem kurd bû. | My teacher was a Kurd. | مامۆستاکهم کوردبوو. |
|---|---|---|
| Hâwrrê kiçekem juân bû. | My girlfriend was beautiful. | هاوری کچهکهم جوان بوو. |
| Min kitêbêki kurdîm hebû. | I had a Kurdish book. | من کتێبێکی کوردیم ههبوو. |
| Ême le dûrewe şâxekânmân bînîn. | We saw the mountains far away. | ئێمه له دووره وه شاخهکانمان بینین |
| Dwênê ême çûyn bo Hewlêr. | We went to Erbil yesterday. | دوێنێ، ئێمه چووین بۆ ههولێر. |

| | | |
|---|---|---|
| Zânkoke le Silêmânî bû. | The university was in Sulaymaniye. | زانکۆکه له سلێمانی بوو. |
| Bâwkim syâsetmedâr bû. | My father was a politician. | باوکم سیاسەتمەدار بوو. |
| Min sî ktêbim heye, bellâm tenhâ sêyânim xwêndotewe. | I had thirty books, but I only read three. | من سی کتێبم هەیه، به لّام تەنها سێیانم خوێندۆتەوه. |
| Pşîlakem hî astenbûle bû. | My cat was from Istanbul. | پشیلەکەم هی ئەستەنبووله بوو. |

## Words and phrases

| | |
|---|---|
| **le dûrewe** | from afar |
| **dwênê** | yesterday |
| **syâsetmedâr** | politician |
| **xwêndinewe** | to read |
| **pşîla** | cat |

## Translate into English.

Min çûm bo gundêk-i biçuk le şâxekân.
Çon bu? We çend xellkî le dezhyâ?
Emâne çutyârî sâde bûn.
Xânwekân sâdebûn bellâm zor xâwên bûn.
Pêşmerge wâtây çîye?
Wâtâ "awân-i rûyân le merge".

**Translate into Kurdish.**

I was at the university on Monday.
You were at the pharmacy on Friday.
Sarkawk went to Hawler on Thursday.
My mother is French, but my father is American.
Qaladze is a small city.
What does genocide mean?
Erbil is far away, and the road is not safe.
In Erbil I had a cat.
My friend was an Arab.
I have five Kurdish friends who help me.
The students were in Erbil.

# Lesson 14 – Religion

John has remarked on the fact that there are mosques everywhere in the Kurdistan Region. Signs of religious activity are found in every town and city. There are also churches in the larger cities and in some districts. The majority of people belong to the Sunni sect of Islam, but there is little sign of the religious strife that exists in some parts of the Middle East. Christians have lived there for centuries, and there are also such indigenous religious groups as the Yezidis, who practice elements of ancient Iranian religion mixed with other traditions. In particular they were influenced by a form of Islamic mysticism introduced in the twelfth century by a Sufi sheikh or religious leader.

## John

| | | |
|---|---|---|
| Wâ pêdeçêt ke mizgewt-i zor le şâr u lâdêkân hebin. | There seem to be many mosques in the towns and villages. | وا پێده چێت که مزگهوتی زۆر له شارو لادێکان ههبن. |

## Sarkawt

Bellê, xellkî zorbey beşekân lêre zor be dînin.

Yes, people here are, for the most, part very religious.

به‌لای ، خه‌لكی زۆربه‌ی به شه‌كان لێره زۆر به دینن.

Lem nâwçeyedâ zorbey kurdekân sunney musullmânin, bellâm le îrân şî'ahen heye.

In this area most Kurds are Sunni Muslims, though in Iran many are Shiite.

له‌م ناوچه‌یه‌دا زۆربه‌ی كورده‌كان سونه‌ی موسولمانن، به‌لام له ئێران شیعه ن هه یه

Âya hîç grupêkî îtir âyînî heye?

Are there other religious groups as well?

ئایه هیچ گروپێكی یتر ئاینی هه یه؟

Bellê. Mesîhyekân bo sedehâ sâll lêre be âştî zhiyâwin.

Yes, Christians have lived here in peace for centuries.

به‌لی ، مه‌سیحیه‌كان بۆ سه‌ده‌ها سال لێره به ئاشتی ژیاون.

Herwehâ xêzân-i êzidîykânîşî lêye.

There are also Yezidi families.

هه‌روه‌ها خێزانی یه‌زیدیه‌كانیشی لێیه .

92

| | | |
|---|---|---|
| Mêzhûyâne, gel-i kurd lêbûrideye, legell eweşdâ kemêk nâkok-i âynî heye. | Historically, the Kurdish people are tolerant, and with that there is little religious friction. | مێژوویانه گه لی کورد لێبووردهیه، لهگهڵ ئهوه شدا کهمێک ناکۆکی ئاینی ههیه. |

## Words and phrases

| | |
|---|---|
| wâ pêdeçêt | it seems |
| mizgewt | mosque |
| zorbey | mostly |
| dînin | religious |
| sunne | Sunni |
| şî'ah | Shiite |
| îtir | other |
| âynî | religious |
| mesîhyekân | Christians |
| âştî | harmony/peacefully |
| sedehâ | hundreds |
| êzidî | Yezidi |
| mêjûyâne | historically |
| gel | people |
| lêburide | tolerant |
| legell eweşdâ | even with that |
| nâkokî | trouble/conflict |

93

# Cardinal numbers 10 to 1,000,000

| | | | |
|---|---|---|---|
| 10 | de | 30 | sî |
| 11 | yâzde | 31 | sî u yek |
| 12 | dwâzde | 32 | sî u dû |
| 13 | sêzde | 33 | sî u sê |
| 14 | çwârde | 40 | çil |
| 15 | pâzde | 41 | çil u yek |
| 16 | şâzde | 50 | pênjâ |
| 17 | havde | 51 | pênjâ u yek |
| 18 | hezhde | 60 | şest |
| 19 | nozde | 61 | şest u yek |
| 20 | bîst | 70 | haftâ |
| 21 | bîst u yek | 80 | hêştâ |
| 22 | bîst u dû | 90 | newed |
| 23 | bîst u sê | 100 | sed |
| 24 | bîst u çwâr | 500 | pênj sed |
| 25 | bîst u pênj | 1000 | hazâr |

| 10,000 | 100,000 | 500,000 | 1,000,000 |
|---|---|---|---|
| de hazâr | sad hazâr | pênj sad hazâr | yek mîlîon |

# Ordinal numbers 1 to 10

| 1st | 2nd | 3rd | 4th | 5th |
|---|---|---|---|---|
| yekem | dûem | sêyem | çwârem | pênjem |

| 6th | 7th | 8th | 9th | 10th |
|---|---|---|---|---|
| şeşem | hewtem | hêştem | nohem | dehem |

**Translate into English.**

Ême degeyne hewlêr, pâytextî herêmî kurdîstân.

Giringtîrîn şiwên sîtâdêle.

Zorbey şâreke zor nwê dête pêş çâw.

Ew peykere bîrewerye gewra çîye ke le ser em
girdeye lewê?

Detîwânîn biçîn be seyâre lêxurîn?

Şemey râbîrdû ême çûyn bo gundêkî biçuk  le
şâxekân.

Dâb u nirîtekân çon bûn lewê?

**Translate into Kurdish.**

There are forty mountains in this region.

There are about twenty three universities in Kurdistan.

How many people live in the village?

There were about twenty families.

This little village had electricity.

The villagers watched television in the evening.

Is Erbil far away?

Nisan is the fourth month.

# Lesson 15 – Women in Kurdish Society

John brings up a very sensitive topic: the question of the position of women in Kurdish society. Sarkawt explains that this is related to deeply ingrained traditional and religious practices. Women in the remote areas sometimes lead difficult lives, much more restricted than those of educated women in the cities. But many Kurdish women in Iraq lead more independent lives than many women in the Middle East. One thing is clear: the situation for both men and women in Kurdish society is changing.

## John

| | | |
|---|---|---|
| Pêge zhinân çîye le komelgâ-i Kurdîdâ? | What is the place of women in Kurdish society? | پێگە ژنان چیە لە کۆمەڵگای کوردیدا؟ |

## Sarkawt

| | | |
|---|---|---|
| Eme pirsyârêk-i ewperî hestyâre. | This is an extremely sensitive question. | ئە مە پرسیاریکی ئەوپەری هەستیاره. |

96

| Komelgâ le mêzhûî dêrîn-i konewe serhelldedâ. | Society is emerging from a deeply traditional history. | کۆمەڵگه له مێژووی دێرینی کۆنه وه سەرهەڵدەدا. |
|---|---|---|
| Jînân le bwârî syâset, râgeyândin u bâzirigânîdâ kâr dakan. | There are women in the fields of politics, the media and business. | ژنان له بواری سیاسه ت ، راگەیاندن و بازرگانیدا کاردەکەن |
| Hukumet çendehâ zânko u xwêndingâ dekâtewe. | The government is opening many universities and schools. | حوکومەت چەندەها زانکۆ و خوێندنگا دەکاتەوه. |
| Le rêgâ-i perwerdewe, hîwâyek heye ke dâb û nerîtekânî pyâwan u zhinân bipârêzirên. | Through [the way of] education, it is hoped that the conditions of men and women will be secured. | لەر رێگەی پەروەردەوه هیوایه هه یه که دابوو نەریته کانی پیاوان و ژنان بپارێزرێن. |

## Words and phrases

| komelgâ | society |
|---|---|
| ewperî | extremely |
| hestyâr | sensitive |
| bekulî | deeply |
| mêzhû | history |
| derîn | ancient, old |

97

| | |
|---|---|
| **kone** | traditional |
| **serhellden** | emerging |
| **bwâr** | field |
| **syâset** | politics |
| **râgeyândin** | media |
| **bâzirigânî** | business |
| **kirdin, ke-** | to make, to do |
| **dewlet, <u>h</u>ukumet** | government |
| **çendehâ** | many |
| **xwêndingâ** | school |
| **kiridnewe** | open |
| **perwerde** | education |
| **dâb u nerîtekanî** | condition |
| **herdû** | both |
| **hîwâ** | hope |
| **parêzrâwe** | secured |

## The verb "to understand"

Present and future forms of the verb "to understand" in the affirmative

| | |
|---|---|
| I understand | tê degem |
| you understand (sg.) | tê degeyt |
| he/she/it understands | tê degat |
| we understand | tê degeyn |
| you understand (pl.) | tê degen |
| they understand | tê degen |

98

Present and future forms of the verb "to understand" in the negative

| I do not understand | tê nagem |
| you do not understand (sg.) | tê nageyt |
| he/she/it does not understand | tê nagat |
| we do not understand | tê nageyn |
| you do not understand (pl.) | tê nagen |
| they do not understand | tê nagen |

## Verbs ending in –ewe

A number of Kurdish verbs end in **-ewe**. Many of them are similar to English verbs with the prefix re- as in *re*peat, *re*turn. Some also have the connotation of opening. Examples: **witinewe**, "to repeat"; **kirdinewe**, "to open". The suffix **-ewe** is added after the personal ending of the verb and does not change.

The present/future indicative of the verb "to open"

| I open | dekâmewe |
| you open (sg.) | dekâytewe |
| he/she/it opens | dekâtewe |
| we open | dekâynewe |
| you open (pl) | dekânewe |
| they open | dekânewe |

## Translate into English.

Rêgâkân betewâwetî selâmet nîn.

Le nêwan rêgâ-i êre u Konyâ, beşêkî qîrnekirâw hebû.

Detwânîn dolekân bibînîn legell lâdêkân u deştekân.

Wâ derdekewê mizgewtî zor le şâr u lâdêkân hebîn.

Mesîhyekân zhîyâwin lêre be âştî bo sedehâ sâll.

Deşt u derî dewru berî Hewlêr zor jwâne.

## Translate into Kurdish.

Many women are in business and politics.

The government is opening schools and universities.

Men and women are now in education.

In Kurdistan there is little religious friction.

Sarkawt opens the door.

We went to the Kurdish restaurant.

We will eat together in the restaurant on the hill.

He is a student at Soran University.

The red dress is mine.

Ali saw your mother at the bazaar.

I do not understand what he says.

# Lesson 16 – Farewell

Sarkawt has accompanied his friend to the modern international airport in Hewler. John will be returning to his home with a whole set of impressions about a region that is extremely complex. He has established a trusting relationship with Sarkawt, and this trust has allowed them to discuss many issues.

## John

| | | |
|---|---|---|
| Min dil tengim be rroyştinim dway em serdâne kurte. | I am sad to be leaving after such a short visit. | من دڵ تەنگم بە ڕۆیشتنم دوای ئەم سەردانە کورتە. |
| Mângêki tewâw besnîye bo têgeyştin le wullâtek-i zor âlloz. | A month is not enough time to understand such a complicated country. | مانگێکی تەواو بە س نیە بۆ تێگەیشتن لە ووڵاتێکی زۆر ئاڵۆز. |

## Sarkawt

| | | |
|---|---|---|
| To degerrêytewe, êstâ dezânî çî detwânî derik pêbikeyt lêre. | You will be back, now that you know what you can find here. | تۆ دە گەڕێتەوە ئێستا دەزانی چی دە توانی دەرک پێبکەیت لێرە. |
| Awe ême le frrokexâne tâzeke-i hewlêrîn. | Here we are at the modern Erbil airport. | ئەوە ئێمە لە فڕۆکەخانە تازەکەی هەولێرین. |

## John

| | | |
|---|---|---|
| Frrokekem hellidestêt le mâwey dû kâtzhimêrdâ. | My plane leaves in two hour's time. | فڕۆکه کهم ههڵدهستێت له ماوهی دوو کات ژمێردا. |
| Min le êstâwe pilân dâdenêm bo geştî dâhâtûm bo enjâm dânî lêkollîneweyek. | I am already planning my next trip back to do research. | من له ئێستاوه پلان دادهنێم بۆ گه شتی داهاتووم بۆ ئهنجام دانی لێکۆڵینهوهیهک |

## Sarkawt

| | | |
|---|---|---|
| Înşâllâ, degerrêytewe. Mâll âwâ. | Inshallah, you will return. Farewell. | انشاللَه دهگهڕێتهوه ، ماڵ ئاوا. |

## Words and phrases

| | |
|---|---|
| **dîl tengim** | I am sad |
| **rroyştin** | to go |
| **serdân** | visit |
| **kurt** | short |
| **mâng** | month |
| **tewâw** | enough |
| **besnîye** | is not |
| **têgeyştin** | understand |
| **âloz** | complicated |
| **wullât** | country |
| **gerrânewe, gerrê-ewe** | to return |
| **derik pêbikeyt** | you find |
| **firrokexâne** | airport |

102

| | |
|---|---|
| **tâze** | modern |
| **firroke** | flight |
| **mâwey** | interval of time |
| **kâtzhîmêr** | hour |
| **hellidestêt** | leaves |
| **le êstâwe** | already, from now on |
| **pilân** | plan |
| **geşt** | trip |
| **dâhâtû** | next |
| **enjâm dân** | to do (research) |
| **lêkolînewe** | research (paper) |
| **mâl âwâ** | farewell |

## Days of the week

| | | | |
|---|---|---|---|
| Saturday | **şemme** | Wednesday | **çwârşemme** |
| Sunday | **yekşemme** | Thursday | **pênjşemme** |
| Monday | **dûşemme** | Friday | **heynî/ jum'a** |
| Tuesday | **seşemme** | | |

## Seasons of the year

| | |
|---|---|
| spring | **behâr** |
| autumn | **xezân/pâyz** |
| summer | **tâwistân/hâwin** |
| winter | **zistân** |

## Months of the year

| | | |
|---|---|---|
| **kânûn-i dûham** | January | كانونى دووەم |
| **şubât** | February | شوبات |
| **âdâr** | March | ئادار |
| **nîsân** | April | نيسان |

103

| | | |
|---|---|---|
| **mays** | May | مايس |
| **ḫuzayrân** | June | حوزةيران |
| **tamûz** | July | تةموز |
| **âb** | August | ئاب |
| **aylûl** | September | ئةيلول |
| **tişrîn-i yekam** | October | تشرينى يةكةم |
| **tişrîn-i dûham** | November | تشرينى دووةم |
| **kânûn-i yekam** | December | كانونى يةكةم |

Note: Not all Kurdîsh speakers use the formal names of the Western months, and they may mix their order. You may find yourself having a conversation about **nîsân**, "April", only to discover that the person you are talking with is speaking about "May". It is sometimes safest to refer to the months by number, "the first month", "the second month", etc.

**Examples**

| | |
|---|---|
| Emro sêşemme. | Today is tuesday. |
| Le kurdistân, yekşemme rozh-i kâre. | In kurdistan, sunday is a work day. |
| Behâr destpêdekat le mângi adar. | Spring begins in april. |
| Dest bekar dekem le mangi eylul. | I begin work in september. |
| Âdâr sêyemin mange. | March is the third month. |
| Nîsân wâtây çîye? | What does **nîsân** mean? |

The traditional Kurdish months of the year following the signs of the zodiac:

| | | | |
|---|---|---|---|
| xâkalêwa | خاکه لێوه | 21- March to 20- April | Aries |
| gullân or bânamarr | گوڵان بانه‌مڕ | 21- April to 20- May | Taurus |
| jozardân | جۆزه‌ردان | 21- May to 20- June | Gemini |
| puşpar | پوشـپه‌ر | 21- June to 21- July | Cancer |
| galâwezh | گه‌لاوێژ | 22- July to 21- August | Leo |
| xarimânân | خه‌رمـانـان | 22- August to 21- September | Virgo |
| rrazbar | ره‌زبه‌ر | 22- September to 21- October | Libra |
| galârêzân or xazałwar | گه‌لاریزان خه‌زه‌ڵوه‌ر | 22- October to 20- November | Scorpio |
| sarmâwaz | سه‌رماوه‌ز | 21- November to 20- December | Sagittarius |
| bafrânbâr | به‌فرانبار | 21- December to 19- January | Capricorn |
| rebandân | رێبه‌ندان | 20- January to 18- February | Aquarius |
| raşame | ره‌شه‌مه | 19 - February to 20- March | Pisces |

## Translate into English.

Pêgî zhînân çîye le komelgâ-i Kurdîdâ?

Komelgâ le mêzhûî derînî konewe serhelldedât.

Kurdekân hendêçâr dellên tâke hawrêyân le jîhândâ şâxekânin.

Dû mîlyon Kurd hellâtin bo şâx be kerekânyân.

Hukumet çendehâ zânko u xwêndingâ dekâtewe.

Wâ pêdeçêt ke mizgewt-i zor le şâr u lâdêkân hebîn.

**Translate into Kurdish.**

I understand a little Kurdish.

I understand some French.

My sister came from Hewler.

I now speak Kurdish with my friends.

Today I am going to America.

That bus went to Sulamaniye.

My mother cannot go to the pharmacy.

I leave at two in the morning.

I will return to Kurdistan, God willing.

When two forms are given for a verb, the first is the infinitive and the second is the stem of the present tense, to which the personal pronouns are added.

| | |
|---|---|
| across | lewberî |
| after | dwây |
| afternoon | dwânîwerro |
| against | dizh |
| airport | firrokexâne |
| almost | nizîki |
| already | peştîr |
| already (from now on) | le êstâwe |
| also | herwehâ |
| also (added to the  end of a word) | -îş |
| America | emirîkâ |
| American | emirîkî |
| among | nêwan |
| ancient | derîn |
| and | we, u |
| Anfal | enfâle |
| April | nîsân |
| Arabic | a'erebî |
| area | nâwçe |
| army | hêz |
| around | dewru berî, lem |
| arrange | rêkxistin, rêkxa- |
| arrive | gayîn, gay- |
| as | weku |
| attractive | serinj-râkêş |

| | |
|---|---|
| August | âb |
| autumn | pâyz, xezân |
| bad | xirâp |
| bazaar | bâzâr |
| be able | twânîn, twân- |
| be glad | xoşhâllin, xoşhâll- |
| beautiful | juân |
| begin | dast + pêkirdin |
| between | nêwan |
| big | gewre |
| black | reş |
| blue | şîn |
| book | kitêb |
| both | herdû |
| boy | kurr |
| bread | nân |
| breakfast | nânî beyânî |
| brother | birâ |
| build | dirusti-kirdîn, ~ ke- |
| building | bînâ |
| bus | pâs |
| business | bâzirigânî |
| but | bellâm |
| buy | kirrîn, kirr- |
| can | twânîn, twân- |
| capital | pâytext |
| car | otombîl, seyâre |
| cat | pşîla |
| certainly | bedîllnyâyewe |
| cherry | gêlas |

| | |
|---|---|
| choose | hellbizhârdin, hellbizher- |
| christian | mesîhî |
| citadel | sîtâdêl |
| city | şâr |
| clean | xâwên |
| clothing | berig |
| cloud | hewr |
| coffee | qâwe |
| cold | sârd |
| colorful | renge u reng |
| come | hâtin, de- |
| come in | were zhûrewe |
| completely | betewâwetî |
| complicated | âloz |
| condition | dâb u nerîtekân |
| conflict | nâkokî |
| country | wullât |
| countryside | deşt u der |
| dark | reş |
| day | rrozh |
| death | merg, mirdin |
| December | kânûn-i yekam |
| deeply | bekulî |
| desire | hez |
| development | geşekirdin |
| difficult | quris |
| do (research) | enjâm dân, ~ dede- |
| doctor | diktor |
| donkey | ker |
| down | xwârewe |

| | |
|---|---|
| dress | kirâs |
| drive | lêxûrrin, lêxûrr- |
| driver | şofêr |
| during | le mâwe-i |
| eat | xwârdin, xo- |
| education | perwerde |
| eight | hêşt |
| eighteen | hezhde |
| eighth | hêştem |
| eighty | hêştâ |
| electricity | kârebâ |
| elementary school | qutâbxâne-i seretâîye |
| eleven | yâzde |
| emerging | serhellden |
| English | înglîzî |
| enough | tewâw |
| even though | herçende |
| evening | êwâre |
| every | hemû |
| excuse me | beyârmertît |
| extremely | ewperî |
| eye | çâw |
| face | rûxsâr |
| family | xêzân |
| far | dûr |
| farewell | mâll âwâ |
| farmer | çutyâr |
| father | bâwk |
| February | şubât |
| few, (a few) | çand, kem |
| field | bwâr, deşt |

| | |
|---|---|
| fifteen | pâzde |
| fifth | pênjem |
| fifty | pênjâ |
| fifty-one | pênjâ u yek |
| find | dozînewe, doz- |
| first | yekem |
| five | pênj |
| five hundred | pênj sad |
| five hundred thousand | pênj sad hazâr |
| flee | hellâtin, hellât- |
| flight | firroke |
| flower | gul |
| food | xwârdin |
| for | le |
| force | hêz |
| fort | qellâ |
| forty | çil |
| forty-one | çil u yek |
| four | çwâr |
| fourteen | çwârde |
| fourth | çwârem |
| French | ferensî |
| Friday | heyni, jum'a |
| friend | hawrrî |
| from | le kwêwe |
| from afar | le dûrewe |
| from here | lêrewe |
| garden | bâx |
| genocide | rreşekuzhî, cînosâyd |
| girl | kiç |
| give | dân, dede- |

| | |
|---|---|
| glass | perdâx |
| go | rroyştin, rro-; çûn, ç- |
| God | xwâ |
| God take care of you | xwâ âgâdârît bê |
| good | bâş |
| good evening | êwâre bâş |
| goodbye | serçâw |
| government | dewlet, hukumêt |
| gray | rreşeke, reses |
| green | sewz |
| happy | şâd |
| harmony | âştî |
| he | ew |
| head | ser |
| headache | sereşe |
| help | yârmetî dân, ~ dede- |
| here | lêre |
| high schools | qutâbxâne-i âmâdeyken |
| hill | gird |
| historically | mêzhûyâne |
| history | mêzhû |
| hope | hîwâ |
| hospital | nexoşxâne |
| hour [of the clock] | sa'ât |
| hour [of time] | kâtzhîmêr |
| house | xânû |
| how | çon |
| how are you? | çonî |
| hundred | sed |
| hundred and one | sed u yek |

| | |
|---|---|
| hundreds | sedehâ |
| hungry | birsî |
| husband | hâwser |
| I | min |
| important | giring |
| in | jurewe, le, le naw, lem |
| in front | pêş |
| in Kurdish | be kurdî |
| in spring | le bahârdâ |
| in the evening | le êwâredâ |
| independent, separate | jyâ |
| intelligent | uryâ |
| intention | nyâz |
| interval of time | mâwey |
| invite | de'awet kirdin, ~ ke- |
| Iraq | a'êraq |
| is not | niye |
| January | kânûn-i dûham |
| juice | şerbet |
| July | tamûz |
| June | huzayrân |
| kebab | kebâb |
| keep | pârâztin, pârez- |
| kilometer | kîlometir |
| know (be familiar with) | nâsin, nâs- |
| know (something) | zânîn, zân- |
| Kurd | kurd |
| Kurdish | kurdî |
| land | zewî |
| late | direng |
| leave | geştin, gel- |

| | |
|---|---|
| left | çep |
| let's go | bâbiçîn |
| like | weku |
| little | biçuk |
| live | zhyân, zhî- |
| long | direzh |
| majority | zorbey |
| many | çendehâ |
| March | âdâr |
| market | bazar |
| married | şwî kirdwe |
| May | mays |
| meal | nân |
| means | wâtây |
| media | râgeyândin |
| milk | şîr |
| million | mîlîon |
| minute | daqîqe, xulek |
| modern | serdemyene, tâze |
| Monday | dûşemme |
| month | mâng |
| monument | bîrewerye |
| morning | beyânî |
| mosque | mizgewt |
| most | zorbe |
| mother | dâyîk |
| mountain | kêw, şâx |
| Muslim | musullmân |
| nation | gel |
| near | nizîk |

| | |
|---|---|
| intention, need | nyâz |
| nearly | nizîki |
| neighborhood | nizîkâne, tenîştîmânewe |
| new | tâze, nwê |
| next | dâhâtû |
| night | şew |
| nine | no |
| nineteen | nozde |
| ninety | newed |
| ninth | nohem |
| no, thank you. | nâ, supâs. |
| none | hiç |
| November | tişrîn-i dûham |
| now | êstâ |
| number | zhimâre |
| October | tişrîn-i yekam |
| of course | bê gumân |
| office | nusînge |
| old | derîn |
| on | le ser |
| one | yek |
| one hundred thousand | sad hazâr |
| one million | yek mîlîon |
| one thousand | hezâr |
| only | take, tenhâ |
| open | kirdinewe, ke-ewe |
| or | yân |
| orange | pirteqâll |
| other | îtir |
| owner | xêwn |

| | |
|---|---|
| park | bâx |
| part, section | beş |
| past | râbîrdû |
| paved | qîrkirâw |
| peacefully | âştî |
| people | xellk |
| Peshmerga | pêşmerge |
| pharmacy | dermânxâne |
| picnic | seyrân |
| place | şiwên |
| plan | pilân |
| please | tikâye |
| please have | fermû |
| politician | syâsetmedâr |
| politics | syâset |
| prettier | şoxtir |
| problem | kêşe |
| progress | pêşkewtin |
| protect | râ-girtin, ~gir- |
| read | xwêndin(ewe), xwêndin- |
| recently | bemduwâyâne |
| recommend | pêşniyâr kirdin, ~ ke- sur |
| red | |
| region | herêm |
| religious | âyînî, dînîn |
| remove, move out | gwâstinewe, gwez-ewe |
| research (paper) | lêkolînewe |
| restaurant | çêşitxâne |
| result | enjâm |
| return | gerrânewe, gerrê-ewe |

116

| | |
|---|---|
| right | rrâst |
| right now | her êstâ |
| river | rubâr |
| road | rêgâ |
| safe | selâmet |
| Saturday | şemme |
| say | gotin, le- |
| school | qutâbxâne |
| second | dûem |
| security | âsâyiş |
| see | bînîn, bîn- |
| seem | dête pêş çâw |
| seems | wâ pêdeçêt |
| sensitive | hestyâr |
| September | aylûl |
| seven | hewt |
| seventeen | havde |
| seventh | hewtem |
| seventy | heftâ |
| sheep | kur |
| Shiite | şî'ah |
| shish | şîş |
| short | kurt |
| should | pewîste |
| sign | nişâne |
| simple | sâde |
| sister | xuşk |
| six | şeş |
| sixteen | şâzde |
| sixth | şeşem |
| sixty | şest |

| | |
|---|---|
| sixty-one | şest u yek |
| smart | zîrek |
| so | boye |
| society | komelgâ |
| soldier | serbâz |
| some [a little] | kemêk |
| some [with plural] | hendê |
| something | hendê şit |
| sometime | hendêjâr |
| speak | qise kirdin, ~ ke-behâr |
| spring | |
| statue | peyker |
| stop | westândin, westen- |
| store | dukân, kogâ |
| street | şeqâm |
| stripe | xet |
| student | qutâbî |
| stupid | gemzhe |
| sugar | şekir |
| summer | hâwin, tâwistân |
| Sunday | yekşemme |
| Sunni | sunne |
| sweet | şirin |
| talk | qise kirdin, ~ ke-çâ |
| tea | |
| teacher | mâmostâ |
| tell me | pêm bille |
| ten | de |
| ten thousand | de hazâr |
| tenth | dehem |
| territory | herêm |

| | |
|---|---|
| thank you | supâs |
| that | ke |
| there | lewê |
| there are | bedî dekrêt |
| there are / is | lêye |
| there was | lêbû |
| therefore | boye |
| thing | şit |
| third | sêyem |
| thirteen | sêzde |
| thirty | sî |
| thirty-one | sî u yek |
| thirty-three | sî u sê |
| thirty-two | sî u dû |
| this | ema |
| three | sê |
| three hundred | sê sed |
| Thursday | pênjşemme |
| tired | mândû |
| to | bo |
| to do, to make | kirdin, ke- |
| today | emrro |
| together | beyekewe |
| tolerant | lêburide |
| tomorrow | sibey |
| top | ser |
| traditional | kone |
| traffic | tirâfîkalâît |
| tree | dâr |
| trip | geşt |
| trouble | nâkokî |

| | |
|---|---|
| try | hewlîdân, hewlîda- |
| Tuesday | seşemme |
| twelve | dwâzde |
| twenty | bîst |
| twenty-five | bîst u pênj |
| twenty-four | bîst u çwâr |
| twenty-one | bîst u yek |
| twenty-three | bîst u sê |
| twenty-two | bîst u dû |
| two | dû |
| two hundred | dû  sed |
| understand | tê-geyştin, tê-ge- |
| valley | dol |
| very | zor |
| victim | qurbânî |
| village | gund, lade, lâge |
| visit | serdân |
| waiter | westâ |
| want | wistîn, we- |
| watch | seyrî kirdin, ~ ke- |
| water | âw |
| weather | keş u hewâ |
| Wednesday | çwârşemme |
| welcome | bâxêrbêy |
| what is? | çîye |
| what was it like? | çon bû |
| where is? | lekwêye |
| white | sipîye |
| wild | siruştî |
| winter | zistân |
| with | legell |

| | |
|---|---|
| woman | zhin |
| work | îş kirdin, ~ ke- |
| world | jîhân |
| year (old) | sâll |
| yes | bellê |
| Yezidi | êzidî |
| you | to |
| you are welcome | şâyânî niye |
| zero | sifir |

## Sorani-English Vocabulary

| | |
|---|---|
| a'êraq | Iraq |
| a'erebî | Arabic |
| âb | August |
| âdâr | March |
| âgâdârît bê | [God] take care of you |
| âloz | complicated |
| âsâyiş | security |
| âştî | harmony, peacefully |
| âw | water |
| âya | introduces a question |
| âyînî | religious |
| aylûl | September |
| bâbiçîn | let's go |
| bâş | good |
| bâwk | father |
| bâx | garden, park |
| bâxêrbêy | welcome |

| | |
|---|---|
| bâzâr | bazaar, market |
| bâzirigânî | business |
| bê gumân | of course |
| be kurdî | in Kurdish |
| bedî dekrêt | there are |
| bedîllnyâyewe | certainly |
| behâr | spring |
| bekulî | deeply |
| bellâm | but |
| bellê | yes |
| bemduwâyâne | recently |
| berig | clothing |
| beş | part, section |
| betewâwetî | completely |
| beyânî | morning |
| beyârmertît | excuse me |
| beyekewe | together |
| biçuk | little |
| bînâ | building |
| bînîn, bîn- | see |
| birâ | brother |
| bîrewerye | monument |
| birsî | hungry |
| bîst | twenty |
| bîst u çwâr | twenty-four |
| bîst u dû | twenty-two |
| bîst u pênj | twenty-five |
| bîst u sê | twenty-three |
| bîst u yek | twenty-one |
| bo | to |
| boye | therefore, so |

| | |
|---|---|
| bwâr | field |
| çâ | tea |
| çand | a few |
| çâw | eye |
| çendehâ | many |
| çep | left |
| çêşitxâne | restaurant |
| çil | forty |
| çil u yek | forty-one |
| cînosâyd | genocide |
| çîye | what is? |
| çon | how |
| çon bû | what was it like? |
| çonî | how are you? |
| çûn, ç- | go |
| çutyâr | farmer |
| çwâr | four |
| çwârde | fourteen |
| çwârem | fourth |
| çwârşemme | Wednesday |
| dâb u nerîtekân | condition |
| dâhâtû | next |
| dân, dede- | give |
| daqîqe | minute |
| dâr | tree |
| dast + pêkirdin | begin |
| dâyîk | mother |
| de | ten |
| de hazâr | ten thousand |
| de'awet kirdin, ~ ke- | invite |
| dehem | tenth |

| | |
|---|---|
| derîn | ancient, old |
| dermânxâne | pharmacy |
| deşt | field |
| deşt u der | countryside |
| dête pêş çâw | seem |
| dewlet, | government |
| dewru berî | around |
| diktor | doctor |
| dînîn | religious |
| direng | late |
| dirusti-kirdîn, ~ ke- | build |
| dizh | against |
| dol | valley |
| dozînewe, doz- | find |
| direzh | long |
| dû | two |
| dû sed | two hundred |
| dûem | second |
| dukân, | store |
| dûr | far |
| dûşemme | Monday |
| dwânîwerro | afternoon |
| dwây | after |
| dwâzde | twelve |
| ema | this |
| emirîkâ | America |
| emirîkî | American |
| emrro | today |
| enfâle | Anfal |
| enjâm | result |
| enjâm dân, ~ dede- | do (research) |

124

| | |
|---|---|
| êstâ | now |
| ew | he |
| êwâre | evening |
| êwâre bâş | good evening |
| ewperî | extremely |
| êzidî | Yezidi |
| ferensî | French |
| fermû | please have |
| firroke | flight |
| firrokexâne | airport |
| geyştin, ge- | arrive |
| gel | nation |
| gêlas | cherry |
| gemzhe | stupid |
| gerrânewe, gerrê-ewe | return |
| geşekirdin | development |
| geşt | trip |
| geştin, gel- | leave |
| gewre | big |
| gird | hill |
| giring | important |
| gotin, le- | say |
| gul | flower |
| gund | village |
| gwâstinewe, gwez-ewe | remove, move out |
| hâtin, de- | come |
| havde | seventeen |
| hâwin | summer |
| hawrrî | friend |
| hâwser | husband |
| heftâ | seventy |

| | |
|---|---|
| hellâtin, hellât- | flee |
| hellbizhârdin, hellbizher- | choose |
| hemû | every |
| hendê | some [with plural] |
| hendê şit | something |
| hendêjâr | sometime |
| her êstâ | right now |
| herçende | even though |
| herdû | both |
| herêm | region, territory |
| herwehâ | also |
| hêşt | eight |
| hêştâ | eighty |
| hêştem | eighth |
| hestyâr | sensitive |
| hewlîdân, hewlîda- | try |
| hewr | cloud |
| hewt | seven |
| hewtem | seventh |
| heyni | Friday |
| hez | desire |
| hêz | army, force |
| hezâr | one thousand |
| hezhde | eighteen |
| hiç | none |
| hîwâ | hope |
| hukumêt | government |
| huzayrân | June |
| înglîzî | English |

| | |
|---|---|
| îş | also (added to the end of a word) |
| îş kirdin, ~ ke- | work |
| îtir | other |
| jîhân | world |
| juân | beautiful |
| jum'a | Friday |
| jurewe | in |
| jyâ | independent, separate |
| kânûn-i dûham | January |
| kânûn-i yekam | December |
| kârebâ | electricity |
| kâtzhîmêr | hour [of time] |
| ke | that |
| kebâb | kebab |
| kem | few |
| kemêk | some [a little] |
| ker | donkey |
| keş u hewâ | weather |
| kêşe | problem |
| kêw | mountain |
| kiç | girl |
| kîlometir | kilometer |
| kirâs | dress |
| kirdin, ke- | to do, to make |
| kirdinewe, ke-ewe | open |
| kirrîn, kirr- | buy |
| kitêb | book |
| kogâ | store |
| komelgâ | society |

| | |
|---|---|
| kone | traditional |
| kur | sheep |
| kurd | Kurd |
| kurdî | Kurdish |
| kurr | boy |
| kurt | short |
| lade | village |
| lâge | village |
| le | for, in |
| le bahârdâ | in spring |
| le dûrewe | from afar |
| le êstâwe | already (from now on) |
| le êwâredâ | in the evening |
| le kwêwe | from |
| le mâwe-i | during |
| le naw | in |
| le ser | on |
| lêbû | there was |
| lêburide | tolerant |
| legell | with |
| lêkolînewe | research (paper) |
| lekwêye | where is? |
| lem | around, in |
| lêre | here |
| lêrewe | from here |
| lewberî | across |
| lewê | there |
| lêxûrrin, lêxûrr- | drive |
| lêye | there are / is |
| mâll âwâ | farewell |
| mâmostâ | teacher |

| | |
|---|---|
| mândû | tired |
| mâng | month |
| mâwey | interval of time |
| mays | May |
| merg | death |
| mesîhî | christian |
| mêzhû | history |
| mêzhûyâne | historically |
| mîlîon | million |
| min | I |
| mirdin | death |
| mizgewt | mosque |
| musullmân | Muslim |
| nâ, supâs. | no, thank you. |
| nâkokî | conflict, trouble |
| nân | bread, meal |
| nânî beyânî | breakfast |
| nâsin, nâs- | know (be familiar with) |
| nâwçe | area |
| nêwan | among, between |
| newed | ninety |
| nexoşxâne | hospital |
| nîsân | April |
| nişâne | sign |
| niye | is not |
| nizîk | near |
| nizîkâne | neighborhood |
| nizîki | almost, nearly |
| no | nine |
| nohem | ninth |
| nozde | nineteen |

| | |
|---|---|
| nusînge | office |
| nwê | new |
| nyâz | intention, need |
| otombîl | car |
| oy | oh |
| pârâztin, pârez- | keep |
| pâs | bus |
| pâytext | capital |
| pâyz | autumn |
| pâzde | fifteen |
| pêm bille | tell me |
| pênj | five |
| pênj sad | five hundred |
| pênj sad hazâr | five hundred thousand |
| pênjâ | fifty |
| pênjâ u yek | fifty-one |
| pênjem | fifth |
| pênjşemme | Thursday |
| perdâx | glass |
| perwerde | education |
| pêş | in front |
| pêşkewtin | progress |
| pêşmerge | Peshmerga |
| pêşniyâr kirdin, ~ ke- | recommend |
| peş | already |
| pewîste | should |
| peyker | statue |
| pilân | plan |
| pirteqâll | orange |
| pşîla | cat |
| qâwe | coffee |

| | |
|---|---|
| qellâ | fort |
| qîrkirâw | paved |
| qise kirdin, ~ ke- | speak, talk |
| qurbânî | victim |
| quris | difficult |
| qutâbî | student |
| qutâbxâne | school |
| qutâbxâne-i âmâdeyken | high schools |
| qutâbxâne-i seretâîye | elementary school |
| râbîrdû | past |
| râgeyândin | media |
| râ-girtin, ~gir- | protect |
| rêgâ | road |
| rêkxistin, rêkxa- | arrange |
| renge u reng | colorful |
| reş | black, dark |
| resesi | gray |
| rrâst | right |
| rreşeke | gray |
| rreşekuzhî | genocide |
| rroyştin, rro- | go |
| rrozh | day |
| rubâr | river |
| rûxsâr | face |
| sa'ât | hour [of the clock] |
| şâd | happy |
| sad hazâr | one hundred thousand |
| sâde | simple |
| sâll | year (old) |
| şâr | city |

| | |
|---|---|
| sârd | cold |
| şâx | mountain |
| şâyânî niye | you are welcome |
| şâzde | sixteen |
| sê | three |
| sê sed | three hundred |
| sed | hundred |
| sed u yek | hundred and one |
| sedehâ | hundreds |
| şekir | sugar |
| selâmet | safe |
| şemme | Saturday |
| şeqâm | street |
| ser | top, head |
| serbâz | soldier |
| şerbet | juice |
| serçâw | goodbye |
| serdân | visit |
| serdemyene | modern |
| sereşe | headache |
| serhellden | emerging |
| serinj-râkêş | attractive |
| şeş | six |
| şeşem | sixth |
| seşemme | Tuesday |
| şest | sixty |
| şest u yek | sixty-one |
| şew | night |
| sewz | green |
| seyâre | car |
| sêyem | third |

| | |
|---|---|
| seyrân | picnic |
| seyrî kirdin, ~ ke- | watch |
| sêzde | thirteen |
| sî | thirty |
| sî u dû | thirty-two |
| sî u yek | thirty-one |
| şîn | blue |
| şî'ah | Shiite |
| sibey | tomorrow |
| sifir | zero |
| sî u sê | thirty-three |
| sipîye | white |
| şîr | milk |
| şirin | sweet |
| siruştî | wild |
| şîş | shish |
| şit | thing |
| sîtâdêl | citadel |
| şiwên | place |
| syâset | politics |
| şofêr | driver |
| şoxtir | prettier |
| şubât | February |
| sunne | Sunni |
| supâs | thank you |
| sur | red |
| şwî kirdwe | married |
| syâsetmedâr | politician |
| tâke | only |
| tamûz | July |
| tâwistân | summer |

| | |
|---|---|
| tâze | modern |
| tâze | new |
| tê-geyştin, tê-ge- | understand |
| tenhâ, | only |
| tenîştîmânewe | neighborhood |
| tewâw | enough |
| tikâye | please |
| tirâfîkalâît | traffic |
| tişrîn-i dûham | November |
| tişrîn-i yekam | October |
| to | you |
| twânîn, twân- | be able, can |
| u | and |
| uryâ | intelligent |
| wâ pêdeçêt | it seems |
| wâtây | means |
| we | and |
| weku | as, like |
| were zhûrewe | come in |
| westâ | waiter |
| westândin, westen- | stop |
| wistîn, we- | want |
| wullât | country |
| xânû | house |
| xâwên | clean |
| xellk | people |
| xet | stripe |
| xêwn | owner |
| xezân | autumn |
| xêzân | family |

| | |
|---|---|
| xirâp | bad |
| xoşhâllin, xoşhâll- | be glad |
| xulek | minute |
| xuşk | sister |
| xwâ | God |
| xwârdin | food |
| xwârdin, xo- | eat |
| xwârewe | down |
| xwêndin(ewe), | read |
| xwêndin- | |
| yân | or |
| yârmetî dân, ~ dede- | help |
| yâzde | eleven |
| yek | one |
| yek mîlîon | one million |
| yekem | first |
| yekşemme | Sunday |
| zânîn, zân- | know (something) |
| zewî | land |
| zhimâre | number |
| zhin | woman |
| zhyân, zhî- | live |
| zîrek | smart |
| zistân | winter |
| zor | very |
| zorbe | most |
| zorbey | majority |

## Materials for Further Study

In the preparation of this text the following three books were very helpful, each in its own way. Because there is no standardized Sorani Kurdish, the vocabularies in the the three books are somewhat at variance with each other. At times one feels one is working in two or three different languages - and in fact that is the case. The language presented here is spoken in the province of Sulaymaniye, but there are many sub-dialects of Sorani even in that smaller region.

W.H. Thackston, (2006) *Sorani Kurdish: Reference Grammar, Selected Readings, and Vocabulary*, from Iranian Studies at Harvard University, retrieved from:
http://www.fas.harvard.edu/ ~iranian/Sorani/index.html

Goddard, Michael. (2007). *English - Kurdish, Kurdish - English, Sorani Dictionary* (Expanded,Revised, and Updated). N.P., Simon Wallenburg Press.

Awde, Nicholas. (2009). *Kurdish Sorani Dictionary and Phrasebook (Romanized) - A language of Iraq and Iran.* New York: Hippocrene Books Inc.

For a more complete treatment of the alphabets in which the Kurdish dialects are written, see the article "Kurdish Alphabets" in the Wikipedia. http://en.wikipedia.org/wiki/Kurdish_alphabets

37479018R00079

Made in the USA
Lexington, KY
03 December 2014